RESEARCH HIGHLIGHTS IN SOCIAL WORK 43

Reconceptualising Work with 'Carers'

Research Highlights in Social Work

This topical series examines areas of particular interest to those in social and community work and related fields. Each book draws together different aspects of the subject, highlighting relevant research and drawing out implications for policy and practice. The project is under the editorial direction of Professor Joyce Lishman, Head of the School of Applied Social Studies at the Robert Gordon University.

The Changing Role of Social Care
Edited by Bob Hudson
ISBN 1 85302 752 9
Research Highlights in Social Work 37

Transition and Change in the Lives of People with Intellectual Disabilities
Edited by David May
ISBN 1 85302 863 0
Research Highlights in Social Work 38

Developments in Short-term Care Breaks and Opportunities
Edited by Kirsten Stalker
ISBN 1 85302 134 2
Research Highlights in Social Work 25

Mental Health and Social Work
Edited by Marion Ulas and Anne Connor
ISBN 1 85302 302 7
Research Highlights in Social Work 28

Planning and Costing Community Care
Edited by Chris Clark and Irvine Lapsley
ISBN 1 85302 267 5
Research Highlights in Social Work 27

Growing Up with Disability
Edited by Carol Robinson and Kirsten Stalker
ISBN 1 85302 568 2
Research Highlights in Social Work 34

RESEARCH HIGHLIGHTS IN SOCIAL WORK 43

Reconceptualising Work with 'Carers'
New Directions for Policy and Practice

Edited by Kirsten Stalker

Jessica Kingsley Publishers
London and Philadelphia

Research Highlights in Social Work 43

Editor: Kirsten Stalker
Secretary: Anne Forbes
Editorial Advisory Committee:

Prof. J. Lishman	Robert Gordon University, Aberdeen
Prof. Ian Broom	Research and Development Office, Grampian University Hospitals NHS Trust
Ms M. Buist	Independent researcher, Edinburgh
Mr P. Cassidy	Formerly Social Work Department Aberdeen City Council, representing the Association of Directors of Social Work
Ms A. Connor	Scottish Human Services Trust
Mr D. Cox	Robert Gordon University, Aberdeen
Prof. M. Hill	University of Glasgow
Prof. G. McIvor	University of Stirling
Dr A. Kendrick	University of Strathclyde
Mr C. Mackenzie	Social Work Department, Aberdeenshire Council
Mr S. McLean	Management Consultant
Dr F. Spencer	Education Department Research Unit, Scottish Executive
Dr A. Robertson	University of Edinburgh

Robert Gordon University
School of Applied Social Studies
Kepplestone Annexe, Queen's Road
Aberdeen AB15 4PH

First published in the United Kingdom in 2003 by
Jessica Kingsley Publishers Ltd
116 Pentonville Road
London N1 9JB, England
and
325 Chestnut Street
Philadelphia, PA 19106, U S A
www.jkp.com
Copyright © 2003 Robert Gordon University, Research Highlights
Advisory Group, School of Applied Social Studies

Library of Congress Cataloging in Publication Data
A CIP catalog record for this book is available from the Library of Congress

British Library Cataloguing in Publication Data
A CIP catalogue record for this book is available from the British Library

ISBN 1 84310 118 1

Printed and Bound in Great Britain by
Athenaeum Press, Gateshead, Tyne and Wear

Contents

Introduction

Kirsten Stalker

Aims of this volume

The aim of the Research Highlights in Social Work series is to bring together the findings of research about a particular topic relevant to social work and, in particular, to make those findings accessible to planners, managers and practitioners. It is some years since an 'anthology' or edited work about carers was published and much has changed during the last decade. Community care, in which carers have always been expected to play a major role, has now had a substantial (although not entirely happy) 'bedding down' period. Many people have left institutions and are being supported in their own homes or in 'homely environments'; fewer people are being admitted to certain types of residential setting. During the same period, carers have become organised on a broader-based platform and in a more sophisticated manner, clearly articulating and publicising their needs. They have gained widespread public sympathy, as well as official recognition, and they have been given formal support, resources and certain legislative rights. Under the Carers' Strategy (DoH 1999), carers' organisations now hold an influential monitoring role in relation to local authorities (Lloyd 2000). Indeed, a case can be argued that carers have increasingly been treated as service providers in their own right and that, to some extent, informal caring has become professionalised.

At the same time, other groups have come to the fore whose needs and demands are different from those of carers, and sometimes in conflict with them. The disability and service user movements have challenged the 'carers' lobby' on various counts, arguing that supporting carers, or treating them as resources, only perpetuates the dependency of disabled people, older people and users of mental health services. Individuals would not have to rely on their families, friends or neighbours for help if the assistance they require was available through formal services or greater provision of direct payments. Indeed, the very notion of 'care' has increasingly been questioned – and rejected by some – since it implies that people need looking after rather than having the right to exercise choice and control over the support they receive and, thus, over other aspects of their lives.

However, while able, articulate and energetic carers and able, articulate and energetic disabled people call for the support they want, there are others who do not or cannot. For a variety of reasons, many carers still make little or no use of formal services and may experience considerable physical, emotional and/or psychological stress as a result. Equally, there are older and disabled people who do not wish to be in charge of their support, who prefer to be looked after by their relatives or who may need advocacy to help them access services or voice their opinions. The competing but urgent needs of these various constituencies and individuals demand and deserve careful attention at both research and policy level. The aim of this volume is to address that demand, but through a critical lens.

The book's perspective

A vast amount of research has been conducted about carers. A striking feature of this literature is the absence of a well-developed critical perspective. Too much has been written about the 'burden' of care rather than the potential rewards. Relationships between carers and those whom they support have often been framed in terms of the dependency of the latter upon the former. Users' views are often missing in research about their care and support: differences between the needs, preferences and rights of carers and users are not always acknowledged. Indeed, some studies of carers seem to have lost sight of the 'other'. Recently, however, some research has focused on the positive aspects of caring, and attention has been drawn to the reciprocity and *inter*dependence which characterise many caring relationships. It is increasingly recognised that physical support need not be coupled to social support. The authors of the chapters in this volume were asked to bring a critical awareness of these issues to their contributions.

Structure of the book

Research on carers has typically examined the topic in terms of carers' characteristics, the characteristics of those whom they support, or the relationships between them (parents, spouses, partners and so on). This book focuses primarily on different aspects of carers' experiences. Some of the chapters include some consideration of past legacies to help explain present frameworks, in terms of knowledge base, policy or practice. Most chapters also highlight constraints in the current policy and practice position. What is perhaps more exciting is that, to varying degrees, all the chapters point to the future, looking at alternative or innovative ways forward, whether in relation to conceptual frameworks, policy and practice developments, ethical dimensions – and/or changes which, in the contributors' judgement, are called for in the light of the research findings they review.

Chapter 1 provides a broad-brush overview of the carers literature, aiming to set the scene for more detailed examination of specific topics in later chapters. It traces the development of carers in social policy research and the various ways they have been counted and categorised. The debates surrounding feminist research on carers in the 1980s and young carers in the 1990s are discussed, along with some possible ways forward.

In Chapter 2, Liz Lloyd argues the need to look beyond 'institutionally created categories of carer and service user' in order to take account of the scope and diversity of caring relationships. She explores the notions of independence and interdependence, the locus of power within relationships and the usefulness of life course perspectives in understanding individual needs. Although caring is often experienced as 'oppressive' by those who need it and 'burdensome' by those who provide it, Lloyd draws on the feminist ethic of care to argue that this does not have to be so.

In Chapter 3, Susan Eley further develops the theme of diversity among carers. Although public policy is predicated on the existence of a 'generic carer' and a 'universal caring experience', she argues that carers differ on many dimensions, including age, gender, ethnicity and place of residence. Eley reviews the research in each area but points out that there is still much that we do not know. In order to meet the needs of 'hidden' carers, and to achieve policy goals, practitioners will have to embrace the diversity that characterises contemporary caring.

The innovative work of Hazel Qureshi and her colleagues at the University of York is having a significant effect on the development of more 'carer-friendly' approaches to assessment. In Chapter 4, Qureshi, Arksey and Nicholas argue that assessment needs to take greater account of individuals' varying circumstances and preferences within the context of different cultures and relationships. They describe the development of outcome-focused approaches to assessment and review for carers which emerged from collaboration with carers, practitioners and managers. Carers have reported that these result in more specific and relevant care plans.

Moving on from assessment, Gordon Grant sets out a compelling case for services to go beyond merely supporting 'caring families'. This chapter focuses on families with disabled children, from whom much can be learnt that is relevant to other carers. Grant urges service planners and providers to recognise, learn from and build on the expertise already within families. He compares this approach with traditional service models which, he suggests, pathologise and marginalise families. He goes on to argue for an ecological model of empowerment which works at individual, and organisational and community levels.

The theme of active participation is developed further in Chapter 6, this time in relation to involving carers in service delivery, planning and evaluation. Helen Rogers and Marian Barnes examine national policy and local practice but caution that consulting carers is not necessarily the same as listening and responding to them. Noting the ambiguous position of carers in relation to service delivery, the authors usefully consider various types of participation and their differing impacts on service development. They conclude, however, that insensitive implementation strategies have often meant that, although carers' needs have changed little over the last twenty years, neither have service responses.

Forty-nine per cent of carers in the UK are in full- or part-time work; 25 per cent are unemployed or economically inactive (the rest are retired). In Chapter 7, Paul Ramcharan and Bridget Whittell review research about the experiences of three groups of carers: those leaving work or reducing their working hours, those balancing work and caring, and those entering, or in some cases re-entering, employment. The authors demonstrate that policy is largely focused on the needs of the second group, with little to support or motivate those not in work to seek employment, thus maintaining the status quo. They argue the need for flexible measures to help more carers find and keep work, located within mainstream employment policy rather than the social care arena, and linked to facilitative social security reforms.

One popular image of carers is of committed selfless souls, while people who abuse individuals in their care may be portrayed as cruel monsters. Somewhere between these two extremes lies a hinterland which is seldom explored. Poor caring or, as Ann Brechin, Rose Barton and June Stein call it, 'care which is not good enough', is the subject of Chapter 8. This, as the authors acknowledge, is 'sensitive and complex territory' in which little research has been carried out and more is needed. The authors describe how, in broaching this area with carers, they were initially 'stuck for words' but came up with the idea of creating six vignettes (reproduced in the chapter), each portraying what might be called an ambiguous caring moment. Carers were asked to discuss their responses. The authors describe this process as 'performing ethics', in which relative 'rights and wrongs' are worked out through dialogue. This chapter also offers useful insights about conducting sensitive research in uncharted waters.

In the final chapter, Margaret Ross sets out the legal framework of caring, drawing out many unresolved dilemmas and potential tensions between users' and carers' interests. Drawing on her detailed knowledge and experience of the law affecting users and carers, she identifies a range of issues of which researchers, planners and practitioners should be made aware. The author highlights the limited understanding of carers within the legal framework supporting and protecting users, and a reluctance among policy makers and practitioners to tackle the legal and ethical challenges carers may face. She calls for more empirical work in this area.

Unfortunately, and despite plans to do so, it did not prove possible to include in this volume a chapter bringing together the findings of international research about carers. Several of the chapters refer to European initiatives promoting good policy and practice and some also draw on international studies. While a good deal of research on carers has been carried out in some countries, such as Scandinavia, Ireland, the United States, Canada and Australia, others appear to be at a much earlier stage. Papers have also been published recently in international journals about informal care giving (or the lack of it) in Japan, South Korea and Israel.

Comparative research provides opportunities for bringing together what is best in different countries and stimulating fresh thinking about social policy (Chamberlayne and King 2000). Research conducted in the European Union during the late 1980s (Jani-LeBris 1993) and in Britain and the 'two Germanies' between 1992 and 1995 (Chamberlayne and King 2000) found that, irrespective of differences in cultural and social patterns, carers adapted to the challenges of their role in similar ways. Families often found it difficult to express their needs and seek formal help, and poor experience of service provision was common (albeit for differing reasons). More recently, a number of European countries have been undergoing similar demographic and policy changes, including the drive to reduce public spending, the shift from institutional to community care and greater priority being given to users' and carers' views. Readers interested in comparative research on carers can turn to Becker (1995, 1999), Becker, Aldridge and Dearden (1998), Bleddyn, Jose and Saunders (1998) or Daly (2000).

Common themes

Although the book covers a wide range of topics related to carers, and embraces a variety of critical perspectives, a number of common themes can be identified from the chapters. At the risk of oversimplifying them, the following summary of cross-cutting themes may be useful in highlighting points that need to be taken into account if a new and more critical understanding of carers is to develop, as well as improvements in policy and practice:

- the lack of theorising about carers; the preponderance of small-scale one-off studies which tend to replicate previous findings

- the many different identities of carers, such as social policy category, object of research, self-advocate, service user, service provider, saint and sinner – illustrating the social construction of the term

- the diversity among carers, both in terms of their own characteristics and the characteristics of those whom they support

- caring relationships are often marked by interdependence. Roles may be fluid or change over time. In assessing individual needs, it is vital to look at each caring relationship as unique, with its own history and dynamics

- the lessons to be learnt from bringing a life-course perspective to the understanding of users' and carers' needs

- there are still pockets of 'hidden' carers – including those from black and minority ethnic communities, older carers and those living in rural areas. In relation to employment policy, carers who do not have paid work remain largely invisible

- there have been some positive developments at policy level over the last decade or so but implementation remains patchy and piecemeal. This is true both at the level of individual support and collective consultation

- service planners and providers should promote active participation by families, building on their particular abilities and personal perspectives, at the level of both individual assessment and wider consultation and involvement

- more attention is needed to outcomes, and the link between process and outcomes. Families should be invited to identify their desired outcomes and goals and both assessment procedures and service delivery should be designed to help them achieve these goals

- policy and practice must be rooted in a firm value base which takes account of both carers' and users' interests. Ethical issues surround and underpin all aspects of caring. How far these are absolute and how far they should be judged in context may not always be clear or agreed. The legal framework of caring, as it currently stands, does not resolve these issues and in some cases raises new ones

- the need and, in some quarters, increasing will to find ways of reconciling or resolving some of the debates and divisions between carers and users, with some possible approaches starting to be identified.

Acknowledgements

As ever, I would like to thank Professor Joyce Lishman, Editor of the Research Highlights series, for her helpful comments during the planning and editing of this book. Thanks are due to Dr Susan Eley of the Department of Applied Social Science at Stirling University for her advice. I am grateful to each of the contributors for their thoughtful chapters – and for submitting their work in good time! Finally, many thanks to Anne Forbes, Secretary to the series, for her invaluable assistance.

References

Becker, S. (ed) (1995) *Young Carers in Europe: An Explanatory Cross-National Study in Britain, France, Sweden and Germany*. Loughborough: Loughborough University.

Becker, S. (1999) 'Carers.' *Research Matters International*, Special Issue, 20–2.

Becker, S., Aldridge, J. and Dearden, C. (1998) *Young Carers and Their Families*. Oxford: Blackwell.

Bleddyn, D., Fernandez, J. and Saunders, R. (1998) *Community Care in England and France: Reforms and the Improvement of Equity and Efficiency*. Aldershot: Ashgate.

Chamberlayne, P. and King, A. (2000) *Cultures of Care: Biographies of Carers in Britain and the Two Germanies*. Bristol: Policy Press.

Daly, M. (2000) *The Gender Division of Welfare: The Impact of the British and German Welfare States*. Cambridge: Cambridge University Press.

DoH (Department of Health) (1999) *Caring about Carers: A National Strategy for Carers*. London: Department of Health.

Jani-LeBris, H. (1993) *Family Care of Dependent People in the European Community*. Dublin: European Foundation for the Improvement of Living and Working Conditions.

Lloyd, L. (2000) 'Caring about carers: Only half the picture?' *Critical Social Policy 20*, 1, 136–150.

CHAPTER I

Carers

An Overview of Concepts, Developments and Debates

Kirsten Stalker

Introduction

This chapter aims to set the scene for the rest of the book, first, by exploring the development of 'carers' in social policy research and the different ways in which the term has been constructed, second, by reviewing key debates in the literature. It begins by tracing the emergence of carers and the carers' movement, along with research about the impact of caring. Estimated numbers and characteristics of carers, and the different ways in which they have been categorised, are reviewed. I also look at the main debates in the literature: that surrounding feminist research published in the 1980s, the response to the 'discovery' of young carers in the 1990s, and the potential conflict between the needs and aspirations of carers and those of the people whom they support. The chapter concludes by looking at some suggested ways forward.

The chapter does not aim to give an account of developments at policy and practice level except where these are relevant to the issues outlined above.

Carers have been defined in different ways at different times. *The Blackwell Encyclopaedia of Social Work* offers the following definition.

> Someone who looks after, or helps look after, a relative, neighbour or friend who has additional needs as a result of disability, illness or ageing.

> The care given is informal in that it does not form part of a paid contract: instead, it relies on a sense of responsibility for, and commitment to the other, driven by feelings of love, duty or concern. (Barton 2000, p.42)

As we shall soon see, however, this apparently straightforward definition is not unproblematic.

The emergence of 'carers'

The term 'carer' barely existed in the English language forty years ago; now it has legal recognition (Bytheway and Johnson 1998). Yet caring – and thus people doing the caring – have existed for centuries. There are literary examples, at least of young carers, such as Dickens's *Little Dorrit* and Hardy's *Tess of the D'Urbervilles* (Aldridge and Becker 1993). However, Bytheway and Johnson (1998), pointing to Townsend's (1957) research into the family life of old people, remind us that, in the mid twentieth century, people supporting relatives or neighbours would not have seen themselves as carers, far less as doing anything different or special. Pahl (1994) notes that the term first appeared in the social care literature during the late 1970s, although not in a dictionary until 1984. Initially, the term '*informal* carers' was widely used to distinguish unpaid support offered by family, friends or neighbours from paid support offered on a more formal basis (Heron 1998). ('Carer' is still sometimes used, in research and practice, to denote a paid helper, which can be confusing.)

Bytheway and Johnson (1998) describe carers as 'a category created through the interplay between individual experience and various interest groups – policy makers, researchers and pressure groups' (p.241). In 1965, The National Council for the Single Woman and her Dependants was set up by the Rev Mary Webster to campaign for single women who found themselves looking after another person, usually a parent. To compensate people forced to give up work in order to look after older relatives, Invalid Care Allowance was introduced in 1975, described as 'the first significant gesture made by central government towards people providing care' (Bythway and Johnson 1998, p.243). However, the exclusion of married and cohabiting women from Invalid Care Allowance (ICA) led to a campaign for its extension, bringing together people who might otherwise have remained isolated from each other and giving them a shared sense of identity and purpose. By questioning the assumption that women care 'naturally' and *should* care rather than undertake paid employment, the campaign had the important effect of politicising the issue of care (Bytheway and Johnson 1998). This was heightened by the fact that, from a rather different perspective, the Disablement Income Group also called for ICA to be extended to married women. As part of this campaign, the Association of Carers was established in 1981 and developed the following definition of a carer: 'Anyone who is leading a restricted life because of the need to look after a person who is mentally or physically handicapped, or ill, or impaired by old age' (quoted in Bytheway and Johnson 1998, p.243).

As the reference to 'a restricted life' suggests, the Association aimed to encourage carers to see their own needs as being as important as those of their relatives. In 1986, the Association merged with what had become the National Council for Carers and their Elderly Dependants to form the Carers' National Association, a substantial pressure group with a wide appeal. ICA was extended to married and cohabiting women in the same year.

Meanwhile, on the policy front, the closure of long-stay hospitals and the growing pressure to support people within their own homes or in the community led to increasing government reliance on informal care provided within the family (DHSS *et al.* 1981, 1984; Griffiths 1988). Assumptions were made about the ability and/or willingness of family members, usually women, to look after their relatives and, to a lesser extent, people's ability and willingness to look after friends and neighbours (but see Abrams *et al.* 1989).

The 'burden' of care

At the same time, research was increasingly focusing on the difficulties faced by carers. A wide range of ill effects was identified as a result of caring. Reviewing this research, Heron (1998) distinguishes between *stress*, involving burn-out, stressful relationships within the family and health problems (see, for example, Briggs and Oliver 1985; Gilhooly 1984; Levin, Sinclair and Gorbach 1989); *limitations*, affecting the quality of day-to-day life, employment prospects, financial matters and missed opportunities for social contacts, relationships and even parenthood (Glendinning 1992; Joshi,1987; Martin and White 1988; Parker 1993; Twigg and Atkin 1994); and *emotional impact* including feelings of being trapped, grief, loss, guilt and anger (Creer, Sturt and Wykes 1982; Gibbons *et al.* 1984; Parker 1990; Thompson and Doll 1982; Ungerson 1987). Research examining the experiences of parents bringing up disabled children also focused on the stresses and strains of everyday life, termed the 'daily grind' by Bayley (1973). The unbalanced picture painted by much of this literature, and its apparent prior assumption that 'a handicapped child makes a handicapped family' (McCormack 1978), was discussed by Byrne and Cunningham (1985) and Baldwin and Carlisle (1994).

The term 'burden' has been widely used in research about carers. It originated in the mental health field to describe the stress experienced by families with a member facing severe and enduring mental health problems (Grad and Sainsbury 1968). Szmukler (1996), writing as a psychiatrist, argues that a 'theoretical vacuum' exists around the term 'burden'. He proposes 'caregiving', 'expressed emotion' and 'family functioning' as alternatives, on the grounds that each is a more neutral term which has a place within psychosocial theory. Heron (1998) describes 'burden' as a negative concept, portraying 'an image of being borne down by a heavy weight' and implying the individual looked after is 'useless' and 'unproductive'. She argues that 'impact' is a more balanced term. Perring, Twigg and Atkin (1990) also suggest 'impact' is preferable, being more objective than 'burden'.

The feminist debate

Among the extensive research published in the late 1970s and 1980s examining the reported stress of caring was a distinctive body of work: the feminist critique of community care or, more precisely, of the underlying assumption that community care was synonymous with care within the family, to be provided mainly by women (Dalley 1988; Finch 1984; Finch and Groves 1983; Graham 1983; Lewis and Meredith 1988; Stacey 1981). These studies again emphasised the demands associated with caring and the negative impact on carers' lives. They identified women's role as carers as part of their oppression and, controversially, some suggested alternative solutions to the 'problem' of looking after 'dependent' people. Finch (1984) argued for a return to residential care while Dalley (1988) proposed 'collective care' to relieve women of their caring roles. This would involve older and disabled people – or anyone requiring ongoing support – living in 'the collective or communal alternative'. Although details of the exact arrangements were left vague, Dalley was suggesting some kind of group home based on the 'highest standards' of existing institutional care. Within this setting, individuals must be responsible for their own life choices; whether they had a choice about moving there in the first place was unclear.

This body of research was fiercely criticised by Jenny Morris and Lois Keith, two disabled feminists (Keith 1990; Morris 1995, 1998). They criticised the research for constructing older and disabled women as 'dependent' and for neglecting their subjective experience. They were particularly scathing of Dalley's call for collective care, arguing that this ignored the rights of disabled women 'to have a home of our own, to live with those we love and who love us, our rights to have children and to bring them up in the way that non-disabled women take for granted' (Morris 1998, pp.164–5).

The Independent Living Movement

Morris (1998) asserts that the disability movement has challenged the concepts of care and caring through its reinterpretation of the notions of dependence and independence. In the sense used by the Independent Living Movement, independence is not about the ability to perform every action by oneself, or to be self-supporting, but rather the ability to exercise choice and control over one's life. It is common for individuals requiring support to be cast in the role of dependants, and thus subordinates. The solution offered by the disability movement is to reduce or dispense with informal care in favour of personal assistants employed by the disabled person, usually through direct payments or Independent Living Fund monies. Research has shown the effectiveness of this kind of support and the high satisfaction among many recipients (Hasler, Zarb and Campbell 2000; Witcher *et al.*

2000). At the same time, Shakespeare (2000a) notes a contradiction between the collectivism of the disability movement and the individualism of its proposed solution to care, suggesting (as discussed later) that this is not the whole answer. Not everyone requiring support wants to employ personal assistants or indeed be responsible for organising help. Equally, while some people do not want to be looked after by their relatives, others prefer to 'keep it in the family' and are resistant to the idea of 'strangers' coming into the home to look after them (Bibbings 1998).

Reciprocity and reward

A further point made by various writers is that many caring relationships are marked by some degree of interdependence or reciprocity (Davis, Ellis and Rummery 1997; Morris 1995; Williams and Robinson 2000). Much of the carers literature identifies one person as giving care and another as receiving it, an 'essentially asymmetric and one to one relationship' (Bytheway and Johnson 1998). This polarisation marginalises other players, ignoring what these authors call the 'multiplicity and reciprocity' of many relationships. It can also imply a dichotomy 'between families with disabled members, and other, 'normal' families. It is suggested that one set of relationships is normal and benign, and the other is problematic and pathological' (Shakespeare 2000, p.55). The person cared for may be a valued family member, making her own contribution through child minding, emotional support or financial help (Heron 1998). Davis *et al.* (1997) cite the example of an older couple, both in poor health, whose son had epilepsy and schizophrenia. When well enough, he cared for them, although there were times when they needed to support him. Williams and Robinson (2000) found that some adults with learning disabilities were taking on caring tasks for older parents. Informal caring takes place within the context of a relationship, good, bad or indifferent (Twigg and Atkin 1994); interpersonal dynamics and histories have a significant impact (Barton 2000). For instance, some couples find that caring roles and activities, particularly the provision of intimate care, can detract from their emotional and sexual relationships (Parker 1993).

More recently, some research has examined the rewards and benefits of caring. Heron (1998) argues that many people gain from caring, especially 'those with a strong nurturing side to their nature', although this observation implies the disabled person serves a useful passive role satisfying someone else's need to nurture. Other examples of positive experiences of caring can be found in Beresford (1994), Lamb and Layzell (1995) and Nolan *et al.* (1996).

The next part of the chapter looks at the extent of caring and different ways in which carers have been categorised in research.

Numbers of carers

There have been debates about the number of carers in the UK and thus the real extent of caring. Estimates vary for a number of reasons, but particularly the way carers are defined and counted which, as Fisher (1997) points out, is a political matter. The first attempt to calculate numbers nationally was made through the General Household Survey of 1985. The data as analysed by Green (1988) suggested there were about six million carers in the UK and that 40 per cent of them were men, flying in the face of previous perceptions that the vast majority of carers were women. About 1.7 million were undertaking care giving for at least twenty hours a week, some for as much as one hundred hours or more. However, the wording of the survey has been criticised both for being subjective, relying on carers to identify themselves and assess 'dependency levels' (Bytheway and Johnson 1998), and over-inclusive in the type of 'caring' task identified (Fisher 1997).

In their secondary analysis of the data, Parker and Lawton (1994) developed a typology of caring activities, constructed by examining the association between different caring tasks. They identified six mutually exclusive categories which took account of combinations of activity. This allowed the authors to distinguish between carers on a number of dimensions. They found that 1.29 million carers had a substantial involvement in providing personal and physical assistance. Parker and Lawton distinguished carers giving this type of support from the larger number of informal helpers who provided practical support as part of a network of helpers in which others carried main responsibility. The authors also differentiated between the tasks undertaken by men and women: women were more likely to be providing personal care, while men were more likely to offer physical (but not personal) care, or practical help only.

The most recent figures available regarding carers in the UK (Rowlands 1998) are derived from the 1995 General Household Survey. These show that one in eight adults, totalling 5.7 million people or 13 per cent of the population, define themselves as carers. Women are more likely than men to be carers but the difference is small – 3.3 million as opposed to 2.4 million. However, women are more likely to carry main responsibility. Fewer people identified themselves as carers in 1995 compared to the 1990 survey, but the latter involved a wide definition. At the same time, the 1995 data reveals evidence of 'continuing "sharpening" of the sharp end of caring' (Rowlands, 1998).

Characteristics of carers

At first, carers tended to be categorised in the literature according to whom, or which community care group, they supported (Twigg 1992a). Claims have been made over the years that looking after people with a particular impairment or condition is in some way distinctive, or more taxing, than looking after others, or that carers in a certain category are less well supported by formal services (see, for example, Twigg and Atkin 1994 on people with learning difficulties; Social Services Inspectorate 1995 on people supporting users of mental health services and very old people; Lamb and Layzell 1995 on disabled people; and Rhodes and Shaw 1999 on carers of people with terminal illnesses). Another approach was to categorise carers according to their relationships to the person they looked after; thus Atkin (1992) reviews the literature on spouse carers, parental carers, filial carers, siblings, child carers and non-kin carers. During the early 1990s, there was a move towards a more generic view (Twigg and Atkin 1994) reflecting the direction of the carers' movement. This in turn gave way to a recognition of diversity among carers themselves.

When carers first emerged as a social policy category they tended to be seen primarily as middle aged, often middle-class women: a number of factors contributing to this perception have already been mentioned.

However, as noted above, the General Household Survey (Green 1988) reported that many men were involved in caring. Arber and Ginn (1989) drew attention to these 'forgotten carers'. Fisher (1997) notes: 'We are so used to conceptualising personal care as women's work that it seems surprising to encounter a man doing it at all, let alone quoting love as the motivation' (p.134).

The issue of male carers is closely bound up with debates about gender and social conditioning. Although there is not room to explore these topics here, assumptions about men's inability or unwillingness to care must be questioned as rigorously as have been assumptions about women's 'natural' propensity to do so. At policy level, the outcome of these debates have important implications for equity in community care provision (Fisher 1997).

It is now recognised that while the largest proportion of carers are middle aged, due to an increasingly ageing population there is also a significant number of older carers. The General Household Survey (OPCS 1992) showed that 27 per cent of people aged over 65 were carers. A higher proportion (14 per cent) of men than women (13 per cent) aged over 65 were carers although, as Fisher (1997) points out, due to women's greater longevity, they were higher in number. The early 1990s saw the emergence of a new category, young carers, which I discuss in more detail below. Another neglected category of carer remains – those living in rural areas (see the chapter by Eley in this volume).

It was not until the early 1990s that attention was drawn to informal care in minority communities (Atkin and Rollings 1992; McCalman 1990). While noting that Asian and Afro/Caribbean carers share many of the same experiences as their white counterparts in terms of demography of care, activities undertaken and receipt of services, Atkin and Rollings (1992) conclude that the position of black carers is made worse by racism and ethnocentric services. More recently, their experiences have been explored by Walker and Ahmad (1994), Gunaratnam (1997) and Chamba *et al.* (1999). While some stereotypes have been exposed, such as the assumption that Asian families invariably 'look after their own' (Baxter 1989), much remains unknown – at least in the literature – about the nature and meaning of caring within minority communities (Gunaratnam 1997). Williams

(2001, p.463) discusses the paucity of attention paid to 'multicultural and racialised contexts of informal care'.

Overall, then, the focus of much carers' research has been on numbers and characteristics, activities, 'burden' and service receipt. The emphasis on these empirical matters has overshadowed attempts to develop a more theoretical understanding of carers. However, a number of attempts have been made to develop typologies of carers, of what they do or why they do it.

Typologies of carers

One of the first was Ungerson's (1987) typology of carers' motivations and position in the life cycle. Today this seems outdated since it distinguishes between men and women on the basis of 'the importance of full-time paid work in men's life cycles' (p.81), while women are classified in terms of motherhood. Ungerson identified different reasons for women taking up caring linked to their biographies.

Twigg (1989) argued that carers occupy an ambiguous position in relation to service provision. As Parker and Lawton (1994) put it, 'they are peripheral to the social care system...yet essential to its functioning' (p.3). Twigg devised a three-point typology in which the dominant model was that of carers as *resources*, taken for granted and perceived only in terms of their ability to support the user. Any conflicts of interest between carer and user are ignored. Where carers are treated as *co-workers*, the main focus remains on the disabled person, but there is a recognition of carers as partners in a joint enterprise and some acknowledgement of possible conflicts of interest. The co-worker model does include an attempt to preserve the carer's well-being but for instrumental reasons, that is, so she can continue caring. Third, carers may be seen as *co-clients*, entitled to support in their own right. The carer's well-being is a valued outcome in itself, and may be 'pursued at the expense of that of the cared-for person, at least in the short-term' (Twigg and Atkin 1994, p.14). A fourth model, added by Twigg (1992b), is the *superseded* carer. Here the aim is not to prop up the caring relationship but to 'transcend' it, either by achieving independence for the disabled person or, when a carer for whatever reason is no longer able to continue, the individual enters a setting which can provide the necessary support.

Twigg and Atkin (1994) developed a typology of carers' responses to their role. *Engulfment* occurs when carers find their lives dominated by supporting the disabled person. Caring becomes their *raison d'être*, to the extent that they cannot stand back nor seek help from services. The authors suggest these are often 'invisible' carers who tend to be at the so-called 'heavy' end of caring. Second, Twigg and Atkin identified a *balancing/ boundary setting* approach adopted by more pragmatic carers ready to ask for help. These people value their autonomy and are not prepared to let caring take over their lives. They are often looking after people with relatively low support needs. The third model is a *symbiotic* one. These carers reap positive benefits from their activities, do not wish to relinquish their responsibility and will only accept help which does not threaten their role as carers. The authors claimed that this model is most common among parents of disabled children.

Most typologies have focused on carers to the exclusion of those on the 'receiving end'. However, in a study of people with learning disabilities and their parents, Walmsley (1996) looked at the caring relationship, which she characterised as *supportive, dependent* or *conflict ridden*, from the perspective of people with learning disabilities. They generally described their relationships with parents as supportive where the latter were 'absent, dead or distant'. Those living with their parents were far more likely to see relationships as dependent or conflictual, leading Walmsley to call on service providers to develop alternatives to family 'co-residence'.

It is worth bearing in mind that no matter how keen researchers may be to name and categorise carers, many people looking after a relative or friend simply do not see themselves in this way. Some do not like the term 'carer' and actively reject it (Heron 1998). Others may never have considered that it might apply to them (Social Services Inspectorate 1995) or find the label intrusive or culturally inappropriate (Barton 2000). Some people have objected to the 'emotional' content of the term, arguing for a distinction between 'caring for' and 'caring about' someone (Parker 1981).

Although Twigg had highlighted a lack of theorising within the literature, and made a start on developing a more theoretical understanding of carers, this was little taken up or developed by other researchers. Instead, in the late 1980s, attention turned towards a 'new' group of carers – children.

The debate surrounding young carers

It has been claimed that 'child carers' have existed since the eleventh century (McLaughlin 1974, quoted in Aldridge and Becker 1993). One of their first appearances in social policy research was in 1988, when Page explored the extent of informal caring by school children in Sandwell. Early estimates indicated there could be 10,000 young carers in the UK but this has risen to a possible 51,000 providing 'substantial' and 'regular' care (Walker 1996). Aldridge and Becker suggest that Bilsborrow (1992) was the first to 'give young carers a voice', since when the subjective experiences of young carers have been a growing area for investigation (Aldridge and Becker 1993, 1994, 1996; Dearden and Becker 1995, 1998; Segal and Simkins 1993; Tucker and Liddiard 1998). These studies have reported that young carers' needs have been largely neglected, that they are denied the rights and opportunities enjoyed by other children and that their caring activities have a series of ill effects, not least on their educational attainment. Aldridge and Becker (1993) have argued that service responses should be guided by a children's rights perspective, enabling young carers to be both children and carers since, the authors claim, that is what most young people in this situation want. Their contribution should be valued and recognised, and appropriate practical and emotional support made available.

The young carers literature evoked a powerful response from other researchers, including disabled activists (Keith and Morris 1995; Olsen 1996; Olsen and Parker 1997). Among the charges were: that the research defined and named a role which did not accord with the young people's own accounts of themselves; that children were portrayed as 'parenting their parents', implying that disabled people are not capable of being 'good' or effective parents; and that the research had fudged the issue of whether or not children should be performing caring tasks in the first place. Keith and Morris (1995) argued that the tasks carried out by young carers may not differ greatly from routine domestic or child-minding chores performed by any children. They criticised young carers research for its neglect of disabling environments and services which, they argued, force some disabled people to rely on their children for support. They were critical of both researchers and the media for suggesting that providing services to young carers is the best way to ease 'the burden of caring'. Rather, the focus should be on

> what needs to be done to prevent parents having to rely on their children for such tasks. In particular, they should focus on how disabled people can access the rights that they already clearly have under existing legislation to practical assistance, aids, adaptations and equipment. (p.54)

Among the points they made in refutation of these criticisms, Aldridge and Becker (1996) rejected the assertion that the young carers literature undermines the parenting skills of disabled adults. Indeed they professed agreement with the disability rights movement that 'the problem lies in disabling environments and services'. Aldridge and Becker differed from their critics, however, in concluding that this problem confirms the importance of researching young carers as a means of drawing attention to their predicament and ensuring they are heard, valued and offered appropriate support.

Conflict between carers and those they support

The debate about the conflicting needs of disabled parents and their 'child carers' has parallels with that between the feminist researchers of the 1980s and their critics. Both are part of a wide-ranging potential conflict between the needs and wishes of carers and those of the people they support. Wood (1991) made this clear when he asserted, for disabled people, 'We don't want care!' while Shakespeare (2000a) characterises the prevailing model of care as 'a colonial relationship'.

It has been suggested that the rise in carers' influence is due in large measure to something of an unholy alliance between researchers and the carers' lobby (Bytheway and Johnson 1998; Keith and Morris 1995) and that carers, at least through their representative bodies, now wield considerable power and influence in relation to service planning and delivery. The Carers' Strategies in England (HMG 1999) and Scotland (Scottish Executive 1999) have given carers' organisations a monitoring role *vis-à-vis* local authorities. Lloyd (2000) argues that the English strategy exemplifies 'the tensions between those who maintain carers' needs are best met through improved services for users and those who support carers' campaign for services in their own right' (p.146).

It has also been argued that the carers' movement has denied relevance to the experiences of individuals being supported (Bytheway and Johnson 1998) and that the campaign for carers' rights has been driven by personal accounts of caring, arguments about the distinctiveness of the caring role, use of emotive terms such as 'burden' and 'restricted' and neglect of the other's experience. Much of the carers literature excludes the users' voice, the implications for them of carers' demands going unexplored. There are exceptions however (for example, Cooney 1997; Walmsley and Reynolds 1998; Williams and Robinson 2001).

Whatever the power held by carers' organisations nationally, evidence (albeit often from studies commissioned or carried out by carers' organisations) shows that many individual carers remain isolated and unsupported, and feel their role is undervalued (Carers National Association 1997; Henwood 1998; Holzhausen 2001; SSI 1995; Warner 1994). There are repeated calls for more support, such as short-term breaks, information, skills training, emotional support, improved communication and problem sharing with professionals, stress management, involvement in planning and delivery of services, and an adequate income (Bibbings 1998; Carers National Association 2000; Fruin 1998; Warner and Wexler 1998).

Lack of services and/or unequal dependencies within the family can reduce the quality of informal support, in some cases leading to poor caring or even abuse (Barton 2000). In a study of informal care for older people (Pritchard 1995), carers reported five factors which 'pushed them over the edge'. These were the older person's behaviour, the caring tasks, frustration, isolation, and lack of services and support. Feeling that they had little or no choice in taking on, or continuing, the caring role can increase the likelihood of abuse (Bibbings 1998). Other risk factors are socially or geographically isolated households, illness or depression in the carer and alcohol consumption (Bibbings 1998). Heron (1998) warns against assuming that the power within a caring relationship always rests with the carer. In relationships with a history of abuse, it may be the carer who is maltreated.

Possible ways forward

Not enough attention has been paid to exploring ways of resolving conflicts between carer and user (Heron 1998). As we have seen, one view is that the answer lies in wider provision of direct payments and personal assistance (Wood 1991). Another is that the best way to support carers is by providing better community services to the individual (Davis *et al.* 1997). On the other hand, treating the two as separate units for assessment, rather than an inter-related whole, may exacerbate conflicts of interest (Davis *et al.* 1997).

Several writers call for a more integrated approach, both at policy and research level. Olsen (2000), discussing the debate on the young carers literature, claims 'the debate has matured and can no longer be seen in simple, dichotomous terms' (p.385). He suggests that researchers are more ready to recognise the potential for disempowerment, for child and adult, if they construct the children of disabled parents as their carers, and have developed a more 'family-based' approach. Similarly, Scottish Office guidance accompanying the 1995 Carers' Act calls for a shift towards an assessment of the 'caring system' and an integrated family approach. Parker (1993) suggests a way forward through action on three fronts. First, acknowledge that disability is socially created: removing the barriers which cause it will reduce the need for care. Second, respect the fact that some people want to have their personal support needs met through informal relationships. Third, recognise informal carers' contribution and offer support to them as well as to users.

Shakespeare (2000a) notes the absence of carers' voices in users' research. Graham (1997) argues that studies of caring need to take account of both sets of literature. While firmly agreeing that the removal of major barriers to inclusion and equality, and the promotion of users' civil rights are vital, Shakespeare (2000a, 2000b) argues there is also a need to recognise the value of interdependence and 'caring solidarity'. He points to a possible way forward in the feminist ethic of care, citing the work of Gilligan (1982), Tronto (1993) and Sevenhuijsen (1998): 'The ethic of care is based on relationships and responsibilities while the ethic of rights is based on rights and rules' (p.60).

The feminist ethic of care (see also Lloyd in this volume) is critical of what it sees as 'male' moral frameworks comprising equality and justice, autonomy and independence, arguing instead for the importance of interdependence. Its proponents point out that, at different times in our lives, we all receive and provide care. Shakespeare has reservations about some aspects of the feminist ethic of care – that it may idealise the caring role and diminish the importance of independence. However, he notes that some writers argue for compatibility between the notions of justice and caring and concludes that the 'crucial move…is to break the link between physical and social dependency' (p.62).

Building on Shakespeare's work, Williams (2001) argues for a 'new political ethic of care' as a counterpoint to New Labour's 'preoccupation' with the ethic of paid work. A political ethic of care would be based on the principle of mutualism, promoting care 'as a social process engendering important elements of citizenship' (p.477). Responding to Shakespeare's concerns about the feminist ethic, Williams suggests that the concept of autonomy should be redefined to accommodate the notion of interdependence. At a practical level, she proposes a national care strategy as an opportunity for 'joined up thinking' bringing together, for example, strategies for supporting specific user groups, for income support, for family, employment and education policies and antidiscrimination measures. Importantly, it would also promote a value base appropriate to informal care, including trust, dignity, mutual respect and bodily integrity.

Summary

Although people have supported or looked after family members over the centuries, it was only in the latter half of the twentieth century that the 'carer' emerged as a social policy category, an object of research and, in some cases, a self-advocate. There is now a huge literature on the 'burden' of caring, although by the late 1980s this research was offering 'diminishing returns' (Twigg and Atkin 1994). It has been counteracted to some extent by studies which have looked at reciprocity and reward within caring relationships.

Overall, the carers literature has been dominated by empirical enquiry, with little well-developed theorising. However, it has not been without its flashpoints – the feminist debate, the young carers debate and the different approaches espoused by the carers lobby and the disability movement. More recently a number of authors have suggested some ways of bringing together these diverse views and interests, recognising the need to remove the social barriers which cause disability, to respect the individual's preferences in relation to the support they receive and to embrace the interdependence which is part of the human condition. Time will tell if any of these options develop and, if so, with what success.

Acknowledgements

Thanks to Tom Shakespeare for his helpful comments on this chapter.

References

Abrams, P., Abrams, S., Humphrey, R. and Snaith, R. (1989) *Neighbourhood Care and Social Policy.* London: HMSO.

Aldridge, J. and Becker, S. (1993) *Children Who Care: Inside the World of Young Carers.* Loughborough: Loughborough University Department of Social Sciences.

Aldridge, J. and Becker, S. (1994) *My Child, My Carer. The Parents' Perspective.* Loughborough: Loughborough University Young Carers Research Group.

Aldridge, J. and Becker, S. (1996) 'Disability rights and the denial of young carers: The dangers of zero-sum arguments.' *Critical Social Policy 16*, 55–76.

Arber, S. and Ginn (1989) 'Men: the forgotten carers.' *Sociology 23*, 1, 111–118.

Atkin, K. (1992) 'Similarities and differences between informal carers.' In J. Twigg (ed) *Carers: Research and Practice.* London: HMSO.

Atkin, K. and Rollings, J. (1992) 'Informal care in Asian and Afro/Caribbean communities: a literature review.' *British Journal of Social Work 22*, 405–418.

Baldwin, S. and Carlisle, J. (1994) *Social Support to Disabled Children and their Families: A Review of the Literature.* Edinburgh: The Scottish Office.

Barton, R. (2000) 'Carers.' In M. Davies (ed) *The Blackwell Encyclopaedia of Social Work.* Oxford: Blackwell.

Baxter, C. (1989) 'Cancer Support and Ethnic Minority and Migrant Communities.' A summary of a research report commissioned by Cancerlink.

Bayley, M. (1973) *Mental Handicap and Community Care.* London: Routledge & Kegan Paul.

Becker, S. Dearden, C. and Aldridge, A. (2000) 'Young carers in the UK: Research, policy and practice.' *Research, Policy and Planning 18*, 2, 7–12.

Beresford, B. (1994) *Positively Parents: Caring for a Severely Disabled Child*. London: HMSO.

Bibbings, A. (1998) 'Carers and Professionals – the Carer's Viewpoint.' In M. Allot and M. Robb (eds) *Understanding Health and Social Care: An Introductory Reader*. London: Sage.

Bilsborrow, S. (1992) *'You Grow Up Fast As Well ... ' Young Carers on Merseyside*. Carers National Association Personal Social Services Society and Barnardos.

Briggs, A. and Oliver, J. (1985) *Caring: Experiences of Looking after Disabled Relatives*. London: Routledge & Kegan Paul.

Byrne, E. and Cunningham, C. (1985) 'The effects of mentally handicapped children on families – a conceptual review.' *Journal of Child Psychology and Psychiatry 26*, 6, 847–864.

Bytheway, B. and Johnson, J. (1998) 'The Social Construction of Carers.' In A. Symonds and A. Kelly (eds) *The Social Construction of Community Care*. London: Macmillan.

Carers National Association (1997) *Still Battling? The Carers Act One Year On*. London: Carers National Association.

Carers National Association (2000) *Caring on the Breadline*. London: Carers National Association.

Chamba, R., Ahmad, W., Hirst, M., Lawton, D. and Beresford, B. (1999) *On the Edge: Minority Ethnic Families Caring for a Severely Disabled Child*. Bristol: The Policy Press.

Cooney, K. (1997) 'Struggles.' In J. Bornat, J. Johnson, C. Pereira, D Pilgrim and F. Williams (eds) *Community Care: A Reader* 2nd edn. London: Macmillan.

Creer, C., Sturt, E. and Wykes, T. (1982) 'The Role of Relatives.' In J.K. Wing (ed) 'Long-term Community Care Experience in a London Borough.' *Psychological Medicine 12*, monograph supplement 2, 29–39.

Dalley, G. (1988) *Ideologies of Caring: Rethinking Community and Collectivism*. London: Macmillan.

Davis, A., Ellis, K. and Rummery, K. (1997) *Access to Assessment: Perspectives of Practitioners, Disabled People and Carers*. Bristol: Policy Press.

Dearden, C. and Becker, S. (1995) *Young Carers: The Facts*. Sutton: Reed Business Publishing.

Dearden, C. and Becker, S. (1998) *Young Carers in the UK*. Loughborough University: Carers National Association in Association with the Young Carers Research Group.

DHSS (Department of Health and Social Security) *et al*. (1981) *Growing Older*. Cmnd 8173. London: HMSO.

DHSS (Department of Health and Social Security) (1984) *Supporting the Informal Carers: Fifty Styles of Caring: Models of Practice for Planners and Practitioners*. London: DHSS.

Finch, J. (1984) 'Community care: developing non-sexist alternatives'. *Critical Social Policy 9*, 6–18.

Finch, J. and Groves, D. (eds) (1983) *A Labour of Love: Women, Work and Caring.* London: Routledge & Kegan Paul.

Fisher, M. (1997) 'Older Male Carers and Community Care.' In J. Bornat, J. Johnson, C. Pereira, D. Pilgrim and F. Williams (eds) *Community Care: A Reader* (2nd edn). London: Macmillan.

Fruin, D. (1998) *A Matter of Chance for Carers? Inspection of Local Authority Support for Carers.* London: Department of Health.

Gibbons, J.S., Horn, S.M., Powell, J.M. and Gibbons, J.L. (1984) 'Schizophrenic patients and their families: A survey in a psychiatric service based on a DGH Unit.' *British Journal of Psychiatry 144*, 70–77.

Gilhooly, M. (1984) 'The impact of caregiving on caregivers: Factors associated with the psychological well-being of people supporting a dementing relative in the community.' *British Journal of Medical Psychology 57*, 35–44.

Gilligan, C. (1982) *In a Different Voice.* Cambridge, MA: Harvard University Press.

Glendinning, C. (1992) *The Costs of Informal Care: Looking Inside the Household.* London: HMSO.

Grad, J. and Sainsbury, P. (1968) 'The effects that patients have on their families in a community care and a central psychiatric service – a two year follow up.' *British Journal of Psychiatry 114*, 265–278.

Graham, H. (1983) 'Caring: A Labour of Love.' In J. Finch and D. Graves (eds) *A Labour of Love: Women, Work and Caring.* London: Routledge & Kegan Paul.

Graham, H. (1997) 'Feminist Perspectives on Caring.' In J. Bornat, J. Johnson, C. Pereira, D. Pilgrim and F. Williams (eds) *Community Care: A Reader* (2nd edn). London: Macmillan.

Green, H. (1988) *General Household Survey 1985 Informal Carers.* London: HMSO.

Griffiths, R. (1988) *Community Care: Agenda for Action.* London: HMSO.

Gunaratnam, Y. (1997) 'Breaking the Silence: Black and Minority Ethnic Carers and Service Provision.' In J. Bornat, J. Johnson, C. Pereira, D. Pilgrim and F. Williams (eds) *Community Care: A Reader* (2nd edn). London: Macmillan.

Hasler, F., Zarb, G. and Campbell, J. (2000) *Implementing Direct Payments: Findings and Policy Issues.* London: Policy Studies Institute.

Henwood, M. (1998) *Ignored and Invisible? Carers' Experience of the NHS.* London: Carers National Association.

Heron, C. (1998) *Working with Carers.* London: Jessica Kingsley Publishers.

HMG (Her Majesty's Government) (1999) *Caring about Carers: A National Strategy for Carers.* London: The Stationery Office.

Holzhausen, E. (2001) '"You can take him home now": Carers' Experiences of Hospital Discharge.' *Carers Health Matters.* Carers National Association, June.

Joshi, H. (1987) 'The Cost of Caring.' In C. Glendinning and J. Millar (eds) *Women and Poverty.* Brighton: Wheatsheaf Books.

Keith, L. (1990) 'Partnerships.' *Community Care*, 22 February.

Keith, L. and Morris, J. (1995) 'Easy targets: A disability rights perspective on the "children as carers" debate.' *Critical Social Policy 44/45*, 36–)57.

Lamb, B. and Layzell, S. (1995) *Disabled in Britain: Behind Closed Doors – The Carers' Experience.* London: Scope.

Levin, E., Sinclair, I. and Gorbach, P. (1989) *Families, Services and Confusion in Old Age.* Avebury: National Institute for Social Work Research Unit.

Lewis, J. and Meredith, B. (1988) *Daughters Who Care: Daughters Caring for their Mothers at Home.* London: Routledge.

Lloyd, L. (2000) 'Caring about carers: Only half the picture?' *Critical Social Policy 20*, 1, 136–150.

Martin, J. and White, A. (1988) *The Financial Circumstances of Disabled Adults Living in Private Households.* London: Macmillan.

McCalman, J.A. (1990) *The Forgotten People.* London: King's Fund Centre.

McCormack, M. (1978) *A Mentally Handicapped Child in the Family.* London: Constable.

Morris, J. (1995) 'Creating a space for absent voices: Disabled women's experiences of receiving assistance with daily living activities.' *Feminist Review 51*, 68–93.

Morris, J. (1998) 'Creating A Space for Absent Voices: Disabled Women's Experiences of Receiving Assistance with Daily Living Activities.' In M. Allott and M. Robb (eds) *Understanding Health and Social Care: An Introductory Reader.* London: Sage.

Nolan, M. Grant, G. and Keady, J. (1996) *Understanding Family Care: A Multi-disciplinary Model of Caring and Coping.* Bucks: Open University Press.

OPCS (Office of Population Censuses and Surveys) (1992) *General Household Survey: Carers in 1990.* OPCS Monitor ss 92/2. London: HMSO.

Olsen, R. (1996) 'Young carers: Challenging the facts and politics of research into children and caring.' *Disability and Society 11*, 1, 41–54.

Olsen, R. and Parker, G. (1997) 'A Response to Aldridge and Becker – Disability rights and the denial of young carers: The dangers of zero-sum arguments.' *Critical Social Policy 17*, 125–133.

Olsen, S. (2000) 'Families under the microscope: Parallels between the young carers debate of the 1990s and the transformation of childhood in the late nineteenth century.' *Children and Society 14*, 384–394.

Page, R. (1988) *Report on the Initial Survey Investigating the Number of Young Carers in Sandwell Secondary Schools.* Sandwell Metropolitan Borough Council.

Pahl, J. (1994) Discovering the Carer. National Institute of Social Work Noticeboard: http:/www.dircsa.org.an/pub/docs/2camp.txt

Parker, G. (1990) *With Due Care and Attention: A Review of Research in Informal Care.* London: Family Policy Studies Centre.

Parker, G. (1992) 'Counting Care: Numbers and Types of Informal Carers.' In J. Twigg (ed) *Carers: Research and Practice.* London: HMSO.

Parker, G. (1993) *With This Body: Caring and Disability in Marriage.* Bucks: Open University Press.

Parker, G. and Lawton, D. (1994) *Different Types of Care, Different Types of Carer: Evidence from the General Household Survey.* London: HMSO.

Parker, R. (1981) 'Tending and Social Policy.' In E.M. Goldberg and S. Hatch (eds) *A New Look at the Personal Social Services.* London: Policy Studies Institute.

Perring, C., Twigg, J. and Atkin, K. (1990) *Families Caring for People Diagnosed as Mentally Ill: The Literature Re-examined.* London: HMSO.

Pritchard, J. (1995) *The Abuse of Older People: A Training Manual for Detection and Prevention.* London: Jessica Kingsley Publishers.

Rowlands, O. (1998) *Informal Care.* Office for National Statistics Social Survey Division. London: The Stationery Office.

Rhodes, P. and Shaw, S. (1999) 'Informal care and terminal illness.' *Health and Social Care in the Community 7,* 1, 39–50.

Scottish Executive (1999) *Strategy for Carers in Scotland.* Edinburgh: Scottish Executive.

Scottish Office (1996) *Carers (Recognition and Services) Act 1995: Policy and Practice Guidance.* Circular SWSG 11/96. Edinburgh: Scottish Office.

Segal, J. and Simkins, J. (1993) *My Mum Needs Me: Helping Children with Ill or Disabled Parents.* Harmondsworth: Penguin.

Sevenhuijsen, S. (1998) *Citizenship and the Ethics of Care: Feminist Considerations on Justice, Morality and Politics.* London: Routledge.

Shakespeare, T. (2000a) 'The Social Relations of Care.' In G. Lewis, S. Gewirtz and J. Clarke (eds) *Rethinking Social Policy.* Bucks: Open University Press.

Shakespeare, T. (2000b) *Help. British Association of Social Workers, Imagining Welfare.* Birmingham: Venture Press.

SSI (Social Services Inspectorate) (1995) *What Next for Carers?* London: Department of Health.

Stacey, M. (1981) 'The Division of Labour Revisited or Overcoming the Two Adams.' In P. Abrams, R. Dean, J. Finch and P. Rock (eds) *Practice and Progress: British Sociology 1950–1980.* London: George Allen & Unwin.

Szmukler, G. (1996) 'From family "burden" to care-giving.' *Psychiatric Bulletin 20,* 449–451.

Thompson, E.H. and Doll, W. (1982) 'The burden of families coping with the mentally ill: An invisible crisis.' *Family Relations: Journal of Applied Family and Child Studies 25,* 3, 379–388.

Townsend, P. (1957) *The Family Life of Old People.* London: Routledge & Kegan Paul.

Tronto, J.C. (1993) *Moral Boundaries: A Political Argument for an Ethic of Care.* London: Routledge.

Tucker, S. and Liddiard, P. (1998) 'Young Carers.' In A. Brechin, A. Walmsley, J. Katz and S. Peace (eds) *Care Matters.* London: Sage.

Twigg, J. (1989) 'Models of carers: How do social care agencies conceptualise their relationship with informal carers?' *Journal of Social Policy 18*, 1, 53–66.

Twigg, J. (1992a) 'Introduction.' In J. Twigg (ed) *Carers: Research and Practice.* London: HMSO.

Twigg, J. (1992b) 'The interweaving of formal and informal care: Policy models.' In A. Evers (ed) *Better Care for Dependent People Living at Home.* Vienna: European Centre.

Twigg, J. and Atkin, K. (1994) *Carers Perceived: Policy and Practice in Informal Care.* Bucks: Open University Press.

Ungerson, C. (1987) *Policy is Personal: Sex Gender and Informal Care.* London: Tavistock.

Walker, A. (1996) *Young Carers and their Families.* London: The Stationery Office.

Walker, R. and Ahmad, W. (1994) 'Asian and black elders and community care: A survey of care providers.' *New Community 20*, 4, 635–646.

Walmsley, J. (1996) 'Doing what Mum wants me to do: Looking at family relationships from the point of view of adults with intellectual disabilities.' *Journal of Applied Research in Intellectual Disabilities (JARID) 9*, 4, 324–341.

Walmsley, J. and Reynolds, J. (1998) 'Care, Support or Something Else?' In A. Brechin, J. Walmsley, J. Katz and S. Peace (eds) *Care Matters: Concepts, Practice and Research in Health and Social Care.* London: Sage.

Warner, L. and Wexler, S. (1998) *Eight Hours a Day and Taken for Granted?* London: The Princess Royal Trust for Carers.

Warner, N. (1994) *Community Care: Just a Fairy Tale?* London: Carers National Association.

Williams, F. (2001) 'In and beyond New Labour: Towards a new political ethics of care.' *Critical Social Policy 21*, 4, 467–493.

Williams, V. and Robinson, C. (2000) *The Carers' Act and Carers of People with Learning Disabilities.* Bristol: The Policy Press.

Williams, V. and Robinson, C. (2001) 'More than one wavelength: Identifying, understanding and resolving conflicts of interest between people with intellectual disabilities and their family carers.' *Journal of Applied Research in Intellectual Disabilities 14*, 30–46.

Witcher, S., Stalker, K., Roadburg, M. and Jones, C. (2000) *Direct Payments: The Exercise of Choice and Control by Disabled People.* Edinburgh: The Scottish Executive.

Wood, R. (1991) 'Care of Disabled People.' In G. Dalley (ed) *Disability and Social Policy.* London: Policy Studies Institute.

CHAPTER 2

Caring Relationships

Looking Beyond Welfare Categories of 'Carers' and 'Service Users'

Liz Lloyd

Introduction

For more than twenty years there has been a vast amount of research on the subject of informal care which has significant implications for the way relationships between service users and carers are understood. Yet much of this has been focused on the separate rights of these two groups, rather than on the relationship between them. In this chapter, I shall use the term 'caring relationships' because I wish to emphasise the point that we need to look beyond the institutionally constructed categories of 'carer' and 'service user' to take account of the scope and diversity of caring relationships.

The chapter begins with a brief outline of research and contemporary perspectives on caring relationships, and will discuss the influence of the policy context. Following this, key themes will be discussed, including independence and interdependence, the nature of power in caring relationships and life course perspectives. There is an emphasis throughout on a relational approach that perceives caring as a normal activity in which we are all implicated in some way or other.

Contemporary perspectives on caring

Feminist, carers' rights and disability rights perspectives on caring relationships have influenced research and policy agendas. Significantly, although
there are overlapping themes, these three have different priorities, present
differing accounts of caring relationships and have, at times, been antago-
nistic (Parker 1993).

Feminist research

In 1978 Hilary Land argued that social policies on family care failed to take
into account the unequal roles of men and women (Land 1978). In the suc-
ceeding years feminist researchers in social policy have argued that community care policy reinforces women's disadvantageous position in the labour
market and thereby prevents them from achieving full citizen rights (see, for
example, Finch and Groves 1983; Graham 1991; Ungerson 1987). Others
consider the impact of caring responsibilities on women's life chances
(Dalley 1996; Lewis and Meredith 1988).

Evidence from the 1985 General Household Survey stimulated a recon-
sideration of earlier feminist assertions because it showed that a large proportion of carers were men (Evandrou 1990; Parker and Lawton 1994).
Commenting on the complex debate about men's and women's roles in
caring relationships, Orme (2001) argues that in feminist traditions men's
role as carers has largely either been denied or has been constructed as in
some way different from the care provided by women. According to Orme,
this position is untenable and a more complex picture of men's and women's
caring capacities needs to be developed.

Finch and Mason (1993) focus on a more micro-level of analysis, examining attitudes towards kinship obligations, the ways in which negotiations
within families give rise to particular roles and commitments and how these
vary. Their findings highlight the importance of understanding human
agency in the development of caring relationships, rather than seeing these
simply as the outcome of men's and women's unequal structural positions.

Carers' organisations

The development of organisations of and for carers has been highly significant in both policy and practice. Bytheway and Johnson (1998) trace the history of the National Council for the Single Woman and her Dependants, since its formation in the 1960s. This body was specifically focused on the needs of single women and Bytheway and Johnson argue that this contributed to the development of contemporary perceptions of the carer as an individual.

Definitions of the term 'carer' vary little and generally refer to the provision of care, help or support to another person who cannot manage on their own because of illness, frailty or disability (see, for example, Caring Matters 2001; DoH 2000; The Princess Royal Trust 2001). However, there is a degree of slippage in the way such definitions are applied. For example, in publications of carers' organisations there are frequent references to the figure of 5.7 million carers in the UK, a figure that derives from responses to the question on caring in the 1985 General Household Survey. Yet it is also widely acknowledged that most carers would not recognise themselves as belonging to the category of 'carer'.

It is therefore open to question how accurately the views presented by campaigning organisations represent the views of carers as a whole. This is an important point to bear in mind when reviewing the research literature on caring. For example, as Evandrou (1996) points out, research findings on carers' health varies according to whether the research was carried out by carers' organisations or used a representative sample, such as the General Household Survey.

The influence of the carers' lobby can be seen in the Government's strategy for carers (Lloyd 2000a). Carers' organisations were actively engaged in the consultation period before its publication and have a role to play in its implementation. The Strategy emphasises the importance of developing services for carers in their own right rather than as a by product of services for the person cared for. It is seen as achieving a better balance between the rights of disabled people and carers by taking into account that carers' needs might not always coincide with those of the service user. The Strategy also refers to carers as service providers, a view that is sometimes referred to as the 'professionalisation' of carers, which will be explored further in this chapter.

Disability researchers

The influence of disabled researchers on contemporary perspectives on caring relationships has also been highly significant. First, the disability rights movement argues for a social model of disability that focuses not on individual impairments and needs related to these, but on the disabling effects of the social and physical environment (Oliver 1990). From this perspective, social policy should concern itself not with the needs of carers but with the rights of disabled people to a physical and social environment, including adequate services.

Second, disabled researchers have challenged the very language of care, arguing that it carries with it connotations of dependency and a lack of autonomy. Sometimes there is therefore a clash of perspectives between those arguing from a disability rights perspective on the one hand and those arguing from the carers' and feminist perspectives on the other. Jenny Morris (1993, 1997), for example, argues that feminists who focus on the burden of caring contribute to the objectification of disabled people.

The disability rights movement has been influential in campaigns for user involvement in, and control over, services (Beresford 1997). The principle that disabled people should be consulted over the development of services is now well established, although this is not always put into practice to the satisfaction of service users. Direct payments, which provide funds for disabled people to employ their own support staff, provide an example of how support can be provided under the control of disabled people. However, it is open to question how widely applicable this is. An amendment to the Direct Payments Act has extended its remit to cover people over the age of 65, but not all older people are willing and able to take up this option (Nocon and Pearson 2000).

Policy influences on caring relationships

The above discussion identifies some of the tensions that exist between organisations of disabled people and carers. It is important to recognise that these tensions are to a large extent an inevitable outcome of the way policies and practices are organised. Barnes (1997), for example, argues that current community care policies have the effect of forcing people into separate and opposing camps. The categorisation of people as 'carers' and 'service users' works against the interests of both groups by distorting the relationship between them and isolating them from wider social life. She points out that some carers object to the practice of conducting separate assessments for carers and service users because it fails to acknowledge the relationship between them.

The process of categorisation also affects personal and social identities. Assuming the identity of 'carer' entitles individuals to recognition and services but at the same time it can have a damaging effect on broader networks of relationships which are not recognised or supported in policy. The concepts of carers and service users, in constant use in the sphere of community care, reinforce the idea that caring relationships are confined to particular categories of individuals. Consequently, caring and the need for care are labelled not as normal but as abnormal human experiences. Indeed, in order to satisfy eligibility criteria for services, the emphasis often needs to be on the abnormal, because in the current context services are focused on those in greatest need.

Despite references to the widespread nature of caring, policies, such as the 1999 Government Strategy for Carers, tend to revert to a narrow focus on particular kinds of carers (Lloyd 2000a). The Strategy promotes the idea that carers are a part of the network of service providers. In so doing, the Strategy contributes to the professionalisation of carers and perpetuates the idea that caring is a one-way activity.

Bowden (1997) notes the pressures created when policies that promote deinstitutionalisation are implemented at the same time that paid employment practices are making it more difficult to offer the kind of care that welfare policy demands. Employed people are required to work longer and more flexible hours to meet the demands of a competitive economy. This contributes to the isolation experienced by many in caring relationships and creates tension and anxiety for employed people, who may be unable to participate in caring in the way they want.

Interdependence and the ethic of care

A key issue to consider is the extent to which a prescriptive policy framework is needed in order to ensure that caring relationships continue. A
number of questions arise. What is the proper role of government in relation
to care? Should the private arrangements of individuals be a matter for
public regulation? Deacon and Mann (1999) argue that 'welfare policy is
either about enabling people to make responsible choices or it is a form of
social engineering' (p.433). The former position suggests that people have a
sense of responsibility for the well-being of others and that this needs to be
fostered and encouraged; the latter that people need to be encouraged or
coerced into behaving in socially responsible ways. An important perspective on these questions has been developed by feminist ethicists. They argue
that it is essential to recognise the moral capacity of individuals to act in
ways that take account of the needs of others. The concrete realities of care
can be understood as people's attempts to act in morally responsible ways.

From this perspective, care is recognised not only as an activity but also
as a moral orientation that challenges masculinist versions of individual
rights and justice in welfare. In her critique of 'Third Way' thinking on
welfare, Sevenhuijsen (2000) argues that interdependence needs to replace
independence and autonomy as the foundation of social policies. She quotes
Tronto (1998) who maintains that: 'The most pressing political discussions
for us have to require us to toss away forever this model of man as a robust,
autonomous, self-contained actor' (p.27).

Instead of understanding caring relationships as the outcome of negotiated obligations between individuals with social rights, the focus needs to
shift to understanding interdependence and caring relationships as the
starting point for understanding individual rights, responsibilities and obligations. Our obligations to others exist as the a priori position and our individual freedoms are negotiated from this point. This is a crucially important
issue in this discussion of caring relationships. It requires a shift of focus from
relationships between carers as individuals on the one hand and service users
as individuals on the other, to understanding the caring relationship as the
basis from which a range of responsibilities is negotiated, including responsibility to oneself.

This conceptualisation has significant implications for both policy and practice. Sevenhuijsen argues:

> A relational approach would start from the idea that policy-making needs elaborated insights into the way individuals frame their responsibilities in the context of actual social practices and how they handle the moral dilemmas that go with conflicting responsibilities of care for 'self, others, and the relationship between them'. (2000, p.11)

The position of feminist ethicists is open to challenge, however. Orme (2001), for example, questions whether their assertion of the superiority of a feminist ethic of care over a masculinist ethic of justice is a fair representation of gender relations in caring. She refers to research that demonstrates men's capacity to care (Fisher 1994; Kaye and Applegate 1994), arguing that this challenges the gendered view that men operate from a set of rules in contrast to women, who act from a sense of duty. This is an important point to bear in mind. However, the 'relational approach' described above by Sevenhuijsen (2000) does not necessarily entail an essentialist understanding of men's and women's attitudes towards caring.

The important point is that our relationships to each other should be understood as fundamental to our individual identity. Moreover, the idea that relationships need to be understood through engagement with everyday social practices has a long pedigree within the social contructionist tradition in sociology (Berger and Luckmann 1967) and is evident in a range of social policy and social work theories.

Orme (2001) also argues that 'care can be oppressive because of the denial of the reciprocity of the caring relationship, whoever provides it' and that contemporary community care policies and practice show how 'care can be reduced to a form of technical oppressive surveillance' (p.23). Thus, we cannot rely on the promotion of care to improve conditions for service users. I would argue, however, that Sevenhuijsen (2000) envisages a different approach to care, in which reciprocity in caring relationships is a central value rather than the version of care that currently underpins social policies. Orme herself stresses the necessity of recognising reciprocity in informal caring relationships in order to avoid an instrumental approach that 'rewards the carer and depends on the passivity and gratitude of the cared for' (p.110).

Thus, Orme also acknowledges, albeit tacitly, the positive potential of care. Williams (2001) discusses the points of tension and agreement between disability rights and the feminist ethic of care perspectives, concluding that social policies need to be developed that would enable us to prioritise opportunities to give and receive care.

The influence of policy on caring relationships has been negative, as already discussed, and it is therefore important to recognise the interrelationships between people's informal, private arrangements for care and the wider public sphere in which discourses of carers and service users circulate. It follows that if caring relationships contribute to the shaping of personal identities, the positive potential of caring needs to be recognised as a positive element in social life and fostered by policy makers.

Towards an integrated approach

This part of the chapter examines the idea of caring networks and critically analyses the concepts of interdependence and reciprocity. A life-course perspective on caring relationships is also outlined. The use of such a model will be essential if practitioners are to engage fully with people's everyday practices in caring relationships and to understand the interconnections between individual, family and social histories.

Caring networks

Examining networks of care enables us to look beyond the popular image of the lone carer and service user. It also highlights diversity in caring relationships (Nolan, Grant and Keady 1996). Wenger (1994) identifies a range of network types among older people which are influenced by family size, patterns of migration and personal characteristics. She argues that the capacity of communities to sustain networks of care is undermined by policies that encourage labour migration and the segregation of older people in special housing complexes. Wenger's conclusions on the effects of migration also have significant implications for families who have come to Britain from other parts of the world. If normal networks of care are disrupted, caring relationships are placed under greater stress.

Bytheway and Johnson (1998) argue that the construction of carers within community care policy and practice has lost sight of the extent and diversity of caring, although evidence of this goes back a long way. For example, Townsend's 'The Family Life of Older People', which shows the many and varied ways in which older people are cared for within families, was published in 1957. Bytheway's own research in South Wales demonstrated that family networks pooled resources at times of need, the most important distinction being whether any individual in the network was in work or not. 'Unemployed, disabled and retired men, along with women and children, were heavily involved in every kind of care' (Bytheway and Johnson 1998, p.252).

A question to be addressed is how the relational approach helps to explain the isolation of many older and disabled people. Some service users' isolation is so extreme, it is difficult to see them as part of a network of care. The point to grasp here is that isolation needs to be understood as the *loss* of networks, the outcome of which is the inability of an older or disabled person to participate in reciprocal or mutual caring. Isolation should be perceived not only as the lack of care provision by families for which community care services are required to compensate but also as an attack on the very identity of the individual concerned. This poses a challenge to service providers to recognise the effect of the loss of social life on the well-being and sense of self of isolated service users and to understand the processes by which their isolation has developed.

Independence, reciprocity and interdependence

A particularly important issue for this discussion is the way that independence is understood. Vernon and Qureshi (2000), for example, point out that, in contemporary policy, independence is defined as the ability to do things for oneself (self-sufficiency) while from a disability rights perspective independence means the ability to exercise control over one's life (autonomy). Both perspectives have significant implications for caring relationships. In contemporary policy, the promotion of independence is an overriding policy aim. As Vernon and Qureshi point out, this is, in practice, the promotion of self-sufficiency – that is, encouraging people to do things for themselves and discouraging their reliance on support services. There is evidence of this approach in the report of the Royal Commission on Long Term Care, which identified how the targeting of services had led to a neglect of older people with carers who were considered to be a low priority (Sutherland 1999).

The concept of interdependence is similarly subject to different interpretations. Morris (1993), for example, refers to 'reciprocity' in relationships where one person is disabled. She recounts disabled people's experiences in which they wanted to feel 'that they were giving something back in return for the help they received from family or friends' (p.87). Morris's research also demonstrates how professional practices failed to take account of disabled people's family networks. Some of the disabled respondents described how they were unable to play their part in family life because they had no access to the kind of support that would enable them to carry out the roles they wished for. One respondent claimed: 'I've not met anybody yet who's involved in these carers' services who is happy giving a service to a disabled person in a family context' (Morris 1993, p.95). This illustrates the point made by Sevenhuijsen (2000) about the need to engage with people's everyday practices.

For Finch and Mason (1993), reciprocity is a highly complex process of exchange, not only in terms of the value of resources and practical help between individuals but also in more diffuse and generalised ways. Giving support and help to a family member is seen as 'the proper thing to do'. However, as Finch and Mason point out, for most people there are limits to reciprocity and a strong sense that relationships should exhibit a balance between dependence and independence. Families sometimes perceived the position of individuals as 'too dependent', and therefore at risk. Those on the receiving end of care also look for balance in relationships. Older people, for example, fear becoming 'beholden' to a relative.

The complex nature of power in caring relationships

Finch and Mason (1993) argue that 'issues of power and control are closely intertwined with the negotiation of the balance between dependence and independence' (p.58). Their findings indicate that people's sense of moral responsibility for their kin is highly variable and that experiencing a sense of moral blackmail was an indication of imbalance in the relationship. Similarly, Twigg and Atkin (1994) describe how some people feel 'engulfed' in their caring roles. Recognising the limits of people's willingness and capacity to care is a vitally important aspect of supporting caring relationships.

Disabled people have argued that the promotion of carers' rights has objectified disabled people, casting them as dependent and not truly adult. From this perspective, care is a wholly negative and oppressive concept. This can be seen in practices such as the sharing of information between professionals and carers to the exclusion of the service user. Orme's (2001) point that care can be a form of oppressive surveillance is relevant in this respect. She argues that informal carers have become professionalised through a series of policy initiatives which have increased their involvement in assessment of older people and people with mental health problems. The portrayal of disabled people as 'burdens' indicates the power of discourses of caring in which sympathy lies with the carer who is obliged to shoulder the burden. The concept of 'respite' for carers illustrates this point. It focuses on the disabled person rather than the broader social context of care services as the source of the carer's problems.

It is also important, however, to acknowledge that the exercise of power within relationships is not a one-way phenomenon. A relational approach enables us to perceive power operating in a more diffuse way. For example, Aitken and Griffin (1996) point out that in abusive relationships it is not always the case that the abused person is dependent on the abuser, as is commonly supposed. At times those who abuse perceive themselves as dependent and it is this that can provoke abusive behaviour. This makes it all the more important that professionals do not focus only on service users but develop a fuller picture of the networks in which they live.

A broader perspective on caring relationships enables us to see how the abuse of power is not confined to the stereotypical 'stressed-out', sole, co-resident carer who cracks under the strain of their responsibilities. While it is essential not to overlook the fact that such situations exist, a broader perspective sheds light on the extent and variations in forms of abuse, including the actions of professionals. Nolan, Grant and Keady (1996), for example, refer to evidence of professional collusion in deceiving older people about going into residential care, presenting it as a temporary measure to save the older person from the grief associated with a permanent move.

A life course approach: Personal histories, futures and transitions

Following Sevenhuijsen's (2000) call for greater awareness of daily practices of the self, we can identify how caring relationships exist in the context of family histories. Daily routines shape our relationships and provide meaning to life in continuous but changing ways throughout the life course.

A historical perspective is essential to understanding how reciprocity works in caring relationships and how people's perceptions of their responsibilities to others is influenced by their social position at different stages in the life course. Finch and Mason (1993) argue that people's present-day experiences of giving and receiving help are shaped by past experiences. Thus, the ability of adult children to offer help to parents in their old age will have been influenced by financial help given by their parents in the past.

Transitions in caring relationships

A life course approach enables us to identify how transitions occur from one stage of life to another. The onset of disease or impairment may trigger significant changes in people's material circumstances, such as living arrangements, employment or finances. The adoption of the identity of carer can be understood as a transition point, often bound up with the need to gain access to benefits and services. 'Becoming a carer' in this sense means perceiving one's activities in a different light and describing them in a different language, a process that is mediated by community care policies and practices.

Even where material circumstances remain relatively unchanged, there will be changes in roles and relationships as, for example, learning disabled children grow into adulthood, or people become more sick and frail through degenerative diseases or develop incapacitating mental health problems.

Aitken and Griffin (1996) point out that in the case of dementia, changes in relationships can be fairly drastic. The role occupied by a spouse or child will alter dramatically in such circumstances, giving rise to the sense that 'looking after such a person may be like looking after a stranger' (p.126). Role change is not, of course, limited to carers. The experience of changed roles for the person with dementia is less well understood but equally needs to be taken into account. Killick and Allan (2001) point out that families might find ways of coping with the symptoms of dementia by distancing themselves from the 'stranger' whose memory loss challenges the foundation of their relationships. However, this can be deeply distressing for the person with dementia who depends on their relationships with those same people to help them retain a sense of identity.

Changes associated with dementia should not always be assumed to be negative. Killick and Allan (2001) have accumulated a number of accounts from relatives and friends of people with dementia of positive developments in relationships through the changes brought about by the disease and the need to communicate in different ways.

Transitions are often anticipated. Parents of children with learning disabilities face the likelihood that their children will outlive them, and need to anticipate their children's need for care in the long term. Their perceptions of the future therefore influence their parenting practices and the wider networks of care. This was brought home to me in a discussion with a mother of a child with learning disabilities. She described how she had decided to use a local residential care unit rather than a foster family for a short break. She felt that this experience would enable her daughter to get used to the idea of residential care and prepare her for the time when she, herself, would be too old to provide care and when she died.

Transition to adulthood is often a very bleak and negative experience for younger disabled people and their families as children's services are brought to an abrupt halt and the inadequacies of adult services are realised. Hirst and Baldwin (1994) found that disabled young people were less likely than their able-bodied counterparts to live independently of their parents. Their social and friendship networks were more circumscribed and they were more dependent on their parents for social lives and leisure activities.

Nolan, Grant and Keady (1996) stress the importance of information for anticipatory care. They note that transition times are often badly handled because family carers are ill-informed about the options for care. They single out, in particular, the transition to residential care of older frail people whose relatives make decisions with little information or guidance, often leaving them with a greater sense of guilt and anxiety. Two important points for practice emerge here. First, while choice is now firmly established as an indicator of good practice in social care, decision making and choice often occur at times when people's capacities for making informed choices are at their weakest. Hoggett (2001), for example, points out that such decisions are often made at times of panic and high emotion when rational action is least likely. Second, transitions to residential care for older or disabled people rarely include a continuing caring role for families. Wright (1998) notes that 'the careers of caregivers do not stop at the institution's door but continue in an altered and still stressful way' (p.87). Again, there is little recognition of the importance of the relationship of the older person to others.

Changing needs over the life course

A life course perspective also enables us to see how needs and levels of independence and dependency fluctuate. Indeed, everyone experiences dependency during the life course, in adulthood as well as infancy. For example, during illness, pregnancy and childbirth and at times of bereavement individuals are dependent on the care and support of others. A life course perspective reminds us of the basic human need for caring relationships, particularly by bringing into focus our mortality. Bauman (1992) refers to death as the ultimate human dependency, since it is at this point that the quest for independence and autonomy becomes a futile exercise.

In recent years I have been engaged in research into approaches to health and social care for older people at the end of life (Lloyd 2000b). This has provided some valuable insights into the relationship between social identity and social relationships. In the course of my research I conducted interviews with community nurses who had experience of caring for older people who died in their own homes. The community nurses felt deeply uncomfortable about the way their relationship with the older person's family came to an abrupt end at the time of death. Not only did this seem to them to be unnecessarily brutal towards the families who were in need of support in their bereavement, it also left them with a feeling that their work with the dead person was not properly finished. The social identity of the older person clearly survived their biological life and a degree of continuity in the relationships between those who had known and cared for them would have acknowledged this.

A life course perspective sheds light on the shortcomings of policy and practice. For example, the Royal Commission on Long Term Care argued that promoting independence rather than care should be the primary aim of long-term care for older people. As they saw it, independence is closer to the ideals of younger disabled people whose views are likely to be more generally representative of older people's in the future (Sutherland 1999). Whilst it is important to take account of new and developing attitudes, this argument fails to recognise that today's younger disabled people cannot represent the views of tomorrow's older disabled people, the majority of whom are not yet disabled in any case. The juxtaposition of old age and disability places people in a different social position from that of youth and disability and this will have an impact on their perspectives on independence, care needs and relationships.

For the older people in my research, independence was not as great a concern as knowing that the people who would be with them in the final stages of life would be familiar to them, would understand their needs and have a caring attitude and excellent skills. Of course, this is not to say that those who are very frail as they approach the end of life can be seen to represent all older people. The key point is that a life course perspective can help us to make better sense of the attitudes, perceptions and experiences of different age groups at different points in time.

Practical and emotional dimensions of caring relationships

Caring relationships are often perceived in familial terms and it is assumed that care within families is of a different order than that provided by paid professionals. Conceptualisations of good professional care emphasise competence, emotional distance and objectivity. Family care, on the other hand, is assumed to be underpinned by feelings of love and not to require high levels of knowledge and competence. Comment on professionalisation of informal carers generally refers to the interruption of bonds of affection and the distancing of carers from those they care for (Fox 1995).

The idea that care within families is satisfactory simply because bonds of affection exist is unsustainable, however, particularly in the current context in which there is greater reliance on informal caring relationships to carry out more and more complex caring activities. There is therefore a need to understand competence in informal caring. For example, Killick and Allan (2001) argue that communication with people with dementia requires particular skills that need to be developed so that the social identity (or 'personhood') of those with dementia is acknowledged and understood. This argument applies in relation to people with other impairments that affect communication.

Competence is also important in terms of the health and safety of individuals in caring relationships. Whilst health and safety are recognised as essential elements of good employment practice, there has been little attention paid to the health of family carers as they take on tasks previously carried out in state institutions (Lloyd 1999). At the same time, it is important to recognise that professional relationships are not inevitably emotionally distant. The community nurses in the example above, who wished to continue their support of bereaved families, demonstrated their emotional involvement, which they saw as inextricably linked to high standards of practice. Therefore, it might be more constructive to see 'professional' and 'familial' categories as representing the opposite ends of a continuum rather than the everyday lived experience of carers. The relationship between paid and unpaid care is, in fact, not dichotomous but closer than is often acknowledged. Thus, care within families requires competence and skill whilst care within the professional sphere requires emotional engagement.

Conclusion

In this chapter I have argued that while under contemporary conditions caring is often experienced as oppressive by those who need it and burdensome by those who provide it, it is possible to envisage a different approach that places caring in a more positive light. By acknowledging interdependence as a normal part of the human condition, we are able to see beyond the narrow conceptualisations of carers and service users that exist in community care policies and practices. From this perspective, care is not regarded as inevitably demeaning to the person who receives it, nor is it necessary to identify a category of carers according to particular criteria. Resources of friendship and support are many and variable and professionals need to engage with people's actual experience in order to practise effectively. This includes recognising that people's capacity to care for others should not be taken for granted and that people's needs for care and support are best met through a combination of resources. Indeed, a life course perspective reminds us that professionals are not immune from the need for care. In the end, caring relationships are exactly what we all need.

References

Aitken, L. and Griffin, G. (1996) *Gender Issues in Elder Abuse.* London: Sage.

Barnes, M. (1997) *Care, Communities and Citizens.* London: Longman.

Bauman, Z. (1992) *Mortality, Immortality and Other Life Strategies.* Cambridge: Polity Press.

Beresford, P. (1997) 'Identity, structures, services and user involvement.' *Research Policy and Planning 15,* 2, 5–9.

Berger, P. and Luckmann, T. (1967) *The Social Construction of Reality.* London: Allan Lane.

Bowden, P. (1997) *Gender Sensitive Ethics.* London: Routledge.

Bytheway, B. and Johnson, J (1998) 'The social construction of "carers".' In A. Symonds and A. Kelly (eds) *The Social Construction of Community Care.* Basingstoke: Macmillan.

Caring Matters (2001) 'What is a carer or caregiver?' http://www.caringmatters.dial.pipex.com/defincarer.html

Dalley, G. (1996) *Ideologies of Caring* (2nd edn). Basingstoke: Macmillan.

Deacon, B. and Mann, K. (1999) 'Agency, modernity and social policy.' *Journal of Social Policy 28,* 3, 413–435.

DoH (Department of Health) (2000) Carers – Government information for carers. http://www.carers.gov.uk/wnaus.num

Evandrou, M. (1990) 'Challenging the Invisibility of Carers: Mapping Informal Care Nationally.' Discussion Paper WSP/49. STICRED, London School of Economics.

Evandrou, M. (1996) 'Unpaid work, carers and health.' In D. Blane, E. Brunner and R. Wilkinson (eds) *Health and Social Organisation: Towards a Health Policy for the 21st Century.* London: Routledge.

Finch, J. and Groves, D. (1983) *A Labour of Love: Women, Work and Caring.* London: Routledge and Kegan Paul.

Finch, J. and Mason, J. (1993) *Negotiating Family Responsibilities.* London: Routledge.

Fisher, M. (1994) 'Man-made care: Community care and older male carers.' *British Journal of Social Work 24,* 659–680.

Fox, N. (1995) 'Postmodern perspectives on care: the vigil and the gift.' *Critical Social Policy 15,* 107–125.

Graham, H. (1991) 'The concept of caring in feminist research: the case of domestic service.' *Sociology 25,* 1, 61–78.

Hirst, M. and Baldwin, S. (1994) *Unequal Opportunities: Growing Up Disabled.* University of York, Social Policy Research Unit.

Hoggett, P. (2001) 'Agency, rationality and social policy.' *Journal of Social Policy 30,* 1, 37–56.

Kaye, L.W. and Applegate, J.S. (1994) 'The family caregiving orientation.' In E.H.J. Thompson (ed) *Older Men's Lives.* Thousand Oaks: Sage.

Killick, J. and Allan, K. (2001) *Communication and the Care of People with Dementia.* Buckingham: Open University Press.

Land, H. (1978) 'Who cares for the family?' *Journal of Social Policy 7,* 3, 357–384.

Lewis, J. and Meredith, B. (1988) *Daughters Who Care: Daughters Caring for Mothers at Home.* London: Routledge.

Lloyd, L. (1999) 'The wellbeing of carers: An occupational health concern?' In N. Daykin and L. Doyal (eds) *Health and Work: Critical Perspectives.* Basingstoke: Macmillan.

Lloyd, L. (2000a) 'Caring about carers: Only half the picture?' *Critical Social Policy 20,* 1, 136–150.

Lloyd, L. (2000b) 'Dying in old age: Promoting wellbeing at the end of life.' *Mortality 5,* 2, 171–188.

Morris, J. (1993) *Independent Lives: Community Care and Disabled People.* Basingstoke: Macmillan.

Morris, J. (1997) 'Care or empowerment? A disability rights perspective.' *Social Policy and Administration 31,* 1, 54–60.

Nocon, A. and Pearson, M. (2000) 'The roles of friends and neighbours in providing support for older people.' *Ageing and Society 8,* 20, 341–367.

Nolan, M., Grant, G. and Keady, J. (1996) *Understanding Family Care: A Multidimensional Model of Caring and Coping.* Buckingham: Open University Press.

Oliver, M. (1990) *The Politics of Disablement.* Basingstoke: Macmillan.

Orme, J. (2001) *Gender and Community Care.* Basingstoke: Palgrave.

Parker, G. (1993) 'A four-way stretch? The politics of disability and caring.' In J. Swain, V. Finkelstein, S. French and M. Oliver (eds) *Disabling Barriers – Enabling Environments.* London: Sage.

Parker, G. and Lawton, D. (1994) *Different Types of Care, Different Types of Carer: Evidence from the General Household Survey.* London: HMSO.

The Princess Royal Trust for Carers (2001) Caring for Carers. http://www.carers.org.uk.

Sevenhuijsen, S. (2000) 'Caring in the Third Way: The relation between obligation, responsibility and care in Third Way discourse.' *Critical Social Policy 20*, 1, 5–37.

Sutherland, S. (1999) *With Respect to Old Age: Long Term Care – Rights and Responsibilities.* Cm 4192–1. London: The Stationery Office.

Tronto, J. (1998) 'Politics, plurality and purpose: How to investigate and theorize care in an institutionalised context.' In T. Knijn and S. Sevenhuijsen (eds) *Care Citizenship and Social Cohesion. Towards a Gender-perspective.* Utrecht: Netherlands School for Social and Economic Policy Research.

Twigg, J. and Atkin, K. (1994) *Carers Perceived: Policy and Practice in Informal Care.* Buckingham: Open University Press.

Ungerson, C. (1987) *Policy is Personal: Sex, Gender and Informal Care.* London: Tavistock.

Vernon, A. and Qureshi, H. (2000) 'Community care and independence: Self-sufficiency or empowerment?' *Critical Social Policy 20*, 2, 255–276.

Wenger, C. (1994) *Understanding Support Networks and Community Care.* Aldershot: Avebury.

Williams, F. (2001) 'In and beyond New Labour: Towards a new political ethics of care.' *Critical Social Policy 21*, 4, 467–493.

Wright, F. (1998) *Continuing to Care: The Effect on Spouses and Children of an Older Person's Admission to a Care Home.* York: Joseph Rowntree Foundation.

CHAPTER 3

Diversity among Carers

Susan Eley

Introduction

Three out of five people living in the UK will have caring responsibilities at some point during their lifetime. Some people may experience being a carer more than once. Contrary to public policy, there is no generic caring experience and no universal carer in society. The diversity of the people who bear the costs (in terms of direct costs and opportunity costs) of personal caring is becoming increasingly less obscured. This chapter will consider diversity among carers: from younger carers under age 11 to older carers, women and men, those from minority ethnic groups and those living in rural areas. This chapter will argue that until the diversity of carers is fully embraced by policy makers, practitioners and social services, 'hidden' carers will not have the freedom and choice to maximise their opportunities in life, to continue caring (if they choose to) safely, with support and without severe financial implications.

The literature on carers can be broadly divided into two bodies of work:

- the early feminist critique of caring that focused on people (understood mainly as women) who care and the 'burden' of caring

- the critique of the early studies which addressed the perspectives of 'other' people who care, challenged the perceived 'burden' of care and stressed the interdependence of caring relationships.

Early studies about carers

The early studies about carers in the 1980s are best remembered for their awareness-raising qualities about the concept and reality of caring (for example, Finch and Groves 1983, Nissel and Bonnerjea 1982, Qureshi and Walker 1989). The legacy of their analytical framework, developed from a primary focus on kin care provided by women carers and the perceived 'burden' of care (for example, Brody 1981, Lewis and Meredith 1988, Nissel and Bonnerjea 1982) has been challenged by academics, practitioners, carers and care-recipients.

Feminist academics have argued that the 1980s literature on caring failed to consider diversity among carers (Graham 1997). The central premises of the early caring literature – carers as primarily white, middle-class, middle-aged women and care being a 'burden' that needed alleviating – led to inadequate and overstated explanations of who cares and why. Graham (1997) argues that issues of 'race' and ethnicity, gender, class, age, sexuality, disability and mental health are crucial structural factors in the experiences of being a carer. Male spouses, sons, children and other older people had no presence as carers in the early literature. This scant description of caring, as Thomas (1993) concludes, offered only a 'partial and fragmented understanding of society's caring activity' (p.667). By focusing on the experiences of a narrow group of kin carers and their perceived 'burden' of care, the early studies also have been criticised for their failure to consider the interdependence between carer and care recipient (for example, Fisher 1997, Morris 1991, 1995, 1997).

The range of carers and caring relationships

Until recently, the diversity of carers has been ignored and many carers' perspectives have been 'on the margins of analysis' (Graham 1997, pp.126–7). Later studies that collected data in the 1990s onwards, or conducted re-analysis of earlier large-scale surveys such as the General Household Survey, have made two major contributions to our understanding of carers and caring. They highlighted the extent of 'other carers' and they demonstrated the interdependence in caring relationships. This chapter will now review recent literature on the diversity among carers and caring relationships. The dimensions of gender, 'race' and ethnicity, residence, age, and income, and some of the additional issues of caring for someone with mental distress and/or disability will be considered below in turn.

Gender

While the 1980s research on caring focused predominantly on women, men were making a significant contribution to caring at that time. Currently, an estimated 42 per cent of carers are men (Department of Health 1999). While women remain (slightly) more likely than men to be carers (Rowlands and Parker 1998), an increase in the proportion of both men and women providing care within the same household was witnessed in the 1990s. Hirst (2001) argues that there were gender differences in the trends of extra-resident and co-resident care during this time. More women than men withdrew from care giving between households and more men than women took on the role of caring for their spouse within the home.

The changing dynamics of employment of men and women in the UK over the last decade has been offered as a partial explanation. Research in Sheffield by Beatty and Fothergill (1999), using survey and in-depth interviewing methods, found in men without paid work that taking on the care of a sick or disabled person in the household (a partner or a child) contributed to their voluntary exit from the labour market. Compared to men who reported that they were 'unemployed', men who described themselves as 'full-time carers' were less qualified, more likely to live in rented housing and to have been out of work longer. The researchers argued that had the male carers' employment chances been greater, they would have bought in caring services in place of providing care themselves (Beatty and Fothergill 1999).

Male carers' perspectives on why they become carers have been explored by qualitative research. Men's voices suggest that they, like some women, become carers 'by default': if they remain in the parental home into later adulthood and a parent becomes unwell or by looking after their partner who becomes in need of care. Men have reported that, in becoming kin carers, they have a sense of 'doing what is right', that it fulfils a wish to 'pay back' the care they themselves have received (Fisher 1994, p.669) and protects other family members from caring responsibilities. This interdependence between male carers and care recipients echoes the literature on women who take on caring responsibilities. Like female carers, the research *with* male carers does not suggest that they perceive caring as a burden (Fisher 1994).

While the assumption remains that co-resident carers are predominantly women, male full-time carers will often remain 'hidden' to support services. Results from a survey of carers' centres across the UK, carried out by Southwark Carers in June 2001, suggests that men are less likely to use support services and may be less likely to identify themselves as carers (Howard 2001, p.7). Existing support services need to acknowledge that there is a sizeable proportion of adult (and probably young) carers who are men. Men's low uptake of support services may indeed reflect a lack of raised consciousness about their caring role in society or, alternatively, may reflect a mismatch between their support needs and the available service provision.

Research with male carers highlights that men and women are both able to 'recognise the need for care, and prioritise social relationships above personal gratification' (Fisher 1994, p.760). Cree (1996) argues that this has importance for social work for two reasons: first to acknowledge the greater equality between men and women as informal carers (p.66) and second to increase tolerance of women who, like men, do not have the capacity to care and choose not to.

'Race' and ethnicity

The recognition of carers from minority ethnic groups is lower than for White carers. Their situation can be made worse by the lack of culturally appropriate services and high levels of unmet needs, social isolation, lack of information and support, poverty and poor housing (Ward 2001). People from minority ethnic groups have tended to be more likely than the general population to be poor, have poorer health and live in deprived areas in overcrowded and unpopular housing (Social Exclusion Unit 2000). Processes of migration, discrimination and exclusion associated with their socioeconomic status may also contribute to differences in mental health (Nazroo 1997; Williams *et al.* 1997). Some chronic and limiting conditions that require care, such as learning difficulties and mental illness, are more commonly reported in different minority ethnic groups than among Whites. A Department of Health report suggests that the prevalence of learning difficulties in people of South Asian origin could be three times higher than in other groups (Mir *et al.* 2001). Levels of mental health concerns also vary across ethnic groups. For instance, the Acheson report on health inequalities stated that depression is more frequently found in African-Caribbeans than Whites (Acheson 1998) and Nazroo (1997) reports that African-Caribbean women have higher rates of diagnosis of psychotic conditions relative to the White population.

The stereotyping of 'caring extended families' and therefore the perceptions of the 'low numbers' of minority ethnic carers in social work has been argued to have contributed to inadequate service provision (Ahmad 2000). It is quite probable that minority ethnic carers may be caring for more than one person at any one time. The high prevalence of learning difficulties in South Asian families has already been noted. Research suggests that in South Asian families containing someone with a learning difficulty, one in five families has more than one member with a learning difficulty and needing care (Mir *et al.* 2001). While some practitioners' notions that communities will 'look after their own' are slow to dissolve, the realities of the extended family structure of South Asian families have been manipulated through occupational mobility, immigration policies and inappropriate housing. Many families struggle to provide significant caring support to parents of disabled children in the community (Ahmad and Atkin 1996). Furthermore, immigration controls and employment patterns have reduced opportunities for Black people to live with their families and care for one another (Tester 1996, p.139).

Qureshi and Walker's (1989) 'hierarchy of care' (p.126) was developed from their study of how both care givers and care recipients perceived caring responsibilities should be met within the (White) family; they produced the following list: '1. spouse (or relative in a lifelong joint household); 2. daughter; 3. daughter-in-law; 4. Son; 5. other relative; 6. non-relative.'

As a concept, the 'hierarchy of care' has a limited value in explaining caring in any family that is not organised on traditional, normative expectations of familial obligations. The concept is unlikely to be relevant to the experience of many minority ethnic groups who may have few or no relatives available to care long-term (Fisher 1994, p.667). In a study of 400 older people, one-third of the Asian respondents and half of the African-Caribbean respondents had no family in Britain (Graham 1997, p.129). Fisher (1994) reported that earlier research indicated that 25 per cent of Asian elders had no close relative living in Britain (p.667). Finch and Mason's (1993) study of 978 adults of all ages living in Manchester between 1985 and 1989 found that a pattern of shared care by relatives and friends was more common among Asian carers and that sons may take the lead in caring for Asian mothers.

Irrespective of ethnicity, the popular image of a Black family has been one of 'families within families, providers of care and social and psychological support' (Patel 1990, p.36). This contributed, with the notion of the extended Asian family, to the assumption that Black and ethnic minority communities do not make use of support services because they desire to 'look after their own' (Gunaratnam 1997, p.116). The 'low numbers' of Black and minority ethnic carers has been considered to be an issue of 'low take-up' rather than need. Gunaratnam argues that the low take-up of caring support services such as home helps, day centres and meals-on-wheels is about culture and tradition as much as it is about lack of information or lack of accessibility of services (Gunaratnam 1997). Within ethnic communities there are significant differences, influenced by factors such as gender, education, income, migration history and the disability of the person requiring care that indicate, Gunaratnam reminds us, a high level of diversity in the caring contexts of Black and Asian families (p.115). In his own study of 33 carers of older Asian people, he found that only 8 of the 33 carers lived in extended, multigenerational families, most elderly couples lived alone in reciprocal caring relationships, while a few family members provided extra-resident care.

Further research with a range of minority ethnic carers is needed to explore the concept of care within their circumstances. The Social Services Inspectorate suggested that 'in order to overcome institutional racism, social services departments should re-think the approach of providing a common service for everyone and treating both black and white older people the same' (Social Services Inspectorate 1999, p.6). Research also suggests that young and younger carers from South Asian communities have similar needs to their White peers but in addition face racism and culturally insensitive services (Shah and Hatton 1999). Black and ethnic minority carers will remain 'hidden' and social work unaware of unmet needs if the context of their caring experiences is incompletely understood and the diversity within families not recognised.

Residence

A further factor that affects carers is residence. Many research studies have frequently assumed that co-residence is an integral part of being a carer (for example, Glendinning 1992) but in a growing number of cases, particularly in caring for an elderly parent, caring is extra-resident, taking place between households. Carers are also differentiated by their residence (and consequently their access to appropriate services) in urban, semi-rural and rural areas. Until the National Strategy for Carers (Department of Health 1999) for England and Wales and the Strategy for Carers in Scotland (Scottish Executive 1999), there were very few services provided for carers in the countryside with the exception of a few high-quality targeted initiatives such as the Norwich and District Carers Forum. Concerning rural carers, there has been little consideration of the practical and personal barriers to seeking support in areas where carers may remain 'hidden' to services but highly visible to community members who may or may not offer support to meet needs (Eley and Lee-Treweek 2001). The caring literature has not given the rural dimension the attention that is deserved. Surprisingly, in the case of rural life literature, most literature has not even considered the role of carers, their inclusion within rural culture or as positive contributors to the regeneration of rural areas.

Mental health

Given the enduring stigma and sidelining of mental health in society, it is not surprising that the published research literature on carers almost totally ignores caring for someone with mental health concerns. While 78 per cent of carers in the General Household Survey (1995) reported that they cared for someone without mental distress, 7 per cent of carers looked after someone with mental health concerns only and 15 per cent of carers looked after someone with physical and mental health concerns.[1] People may avoid services for fear of labelling and subsequent discrimination and social exclusion. Services that are attempted to be accessed by carers of someone with mental distress may not always be available, for instance if a crisis arises at a weekend. Service providers may not always be sympathetic to intervening to support a relative who is a 'hidden' carer (Howe 1999). A Department of Health review of studies about families who cared for relatives with mental distress frequently reported that they often felt they had taken on too much or were unsupported (Department of Health 1998).

Compared to carers of people with physical health issues, carers of people with mental health concerns may have erratic intensive episodes of caring which may have costs to the carer in terms of disruption of all areas of their life. While there is likely to be a range of carer perspectives of caring for someone with mental distress, it is certain that as a type of carer they add to the diversity of caring experiences. Being a carer of someone with mental distress may mean that a person offers support and encouragement as well as helping with finances, dealing with officials and often supervising medication (Harvey 2001) rather than undertaking the physical tasks that are often considered synonymous with being a carer.

Age

People can be a carer at any time in their life. Generally the research literature has struggled with the realities of the diversity of caring experiences of carers and care recipients in relation to age. The following sections highlight the literature within the broad categories of young carers, parent carers, working-age carers and those over pension age.

YOUNG CARERS

Becker *et al.* (1998) describe young carers as 'young people under 18 who provide care to another family member with a physical illness or disability, mental ill health, a sensory disability, who misuses alcohol or drugs or who is frail'. From UK government surveys, it has been estimated that between 0.27 per cent and 0.72 per cent in the 8–17 age group are providing substantial or regular care, that is, more than 20 hours per week.[2] However, there is no universally accepted definition of what constitutes 'providing care'. There is widespread agreement that involvement in particular forms and levels of caring can have a restrictive or negative impact on childhood. There is concern about children who take on responsibility for meeting 'critical' needs, that is, where the person needs help with unexpected and unpredictable frequency, as well as those who are providing regular care. Whatever the level or nature of the care provided, researchers argue that it is the impact of caring on the child's development and opportunities which determines the need for support. The range of needs identified in qualitative research includes social, emotional, educational and health needs.

Young carers have often been conceptualised as 'adults before their time', teenagers burdened with the care of a (stereotypical) disabled parent and having their schooling and leisure opportunities curtailed. A substantial body of the young carers literature has failed to describe the experiences of young carers under the age of 11, to acknowledge that young caring is not a 'one-way street' within families and that the cared for do not abstain from parenting (Wates 2000).

There are problems with estimating numbers of young carers (under 18 years) and younger carers (aged 18–25 years) partly because of the 'private' nature of the caring activity at home and partly because of assumptions about 'caring' activities. Many definitions applied to young and younger carers are relative and assume that they are undertaking physical and emotional tasks that either other children and young people of their age do not do for their family members or that no child or young person should be doing at their age and in their circumstances. The diversity of experiences and availability of other kinds of help, particularly in lower-income and rural families, is largely ignored in the literature which has mainly concentrated on researching opportunistic samples of young carers who are existing service users.

YOUNG CARERS OF DISABLED PARENTS

The dominant research literature on the 'plight' of young carers and the long-term impact on their lives (for example, Aldridge and Becker 1993,

1996; Becker, Aldridge and Dearden 1998; Dearden and Becker 2001; Heron 1998) maintains its influence over the policy agenda. This substantial body of evidence fails to appreciate the complex and diverse reciprocal caring relationships among families (Morris 1997; Olsen 1996) and its rhetoric contributes to the low take-up of support services. The Social Services Inspectorate report found in cases of young carers of disabled parents in all of the councils visited, some people did not wish to be referred to social workers because they were scared that there would be a difference of view about caring activities undertaken by children and young people and scared that their children would be taken away into residential or foster care (Goodinge 2000). The inspection teams also reported that childcare teams in social services departments did not necessarily record that parents had a disability and adult service teams did not routinely record whether there were children in the family (Goodinge 2000).

The interdependence of disabled people as parents and their sons and daughters as carers has been rarely considered in the caring literature. Disability commentators have argued that, in the case of young carers of disabled parents, this has led to the neglect of developing sensitive support services that acknowledge disabled people in their parenting role (Wates 1997, 2000).

PARENT CARERS

Half a million children and young people in the UK have some form of disability and/or long-term illness, of which 170,000 have severe disability. Fourteen per cent of carers are looking after a disabled child or young adult (Howard 2001, p.65). A national survey of (predominantly White) parents caring for disabled children in 1995 found that, compared to other working-age carers, parents were less likely to work because of their caring responsibilities and many incurred additional costs, such as for laundry, bedding and heating. Nine out of ten lone parents and over one-third of couples had no income other than benefits. Many parents (over one-third of the sample), said that their disabled children had needs that they could not meet (Beresford 1995). A later parallel study of a range of minority ethnic families caring for a severely disabled child found even lower incomes and higher costs (Chamba *et al.* 1999). Social work and other voluntary support services must take account of this group's needs as both carers and parents. Recent research suggests that parents of a disabled child may struggle to find appropriate support services that take a holistic view of the family's needs. In this research, parent carers voiced their experiences of prejudice and insensitivity in service provision (Dobson *et al.* 2001). The National Childcare Strategy and its £4 million funds for disabled children[3] offers an opportunity for the development of service provision in consultation with parent carers in England and Wales.

INCOME AND OTHER WORKING-AGE CARERS

Being an adult carer of working age will have a significant impact on how, when and where paid work is taken up. Compared to other parents, parent carers of disabled children are less likely to do paid work outside the home. Many other working-age carers are unable to work when providing care. The Caring on the Breadline survey found that seven out of ten carers under age 50, and nearly eight out of ten carers between age 56 and 60, had given up work to care (Holzhausen and Pearlman 2000). A high proportion (87 per cent) of the working-age carers who responded to the survey questions said that they felt worse off than older carers did.

Income plays a key role in differentiating who cares and the extent and type of caring that working-age carers do. Research carried out for the Department of Social Security highlights that 26 per cent of workless couples cared for someone other than their own children because of illness or disability (79 per cent of these were caring for their partner) compared to 10 per cent of couples with 'moderate' incomes[4] (Marsh *et al.* 2001). Nine per cent of lone parents had additional caring responsibilities as well as looking after their own children, and 10 per cent of non-working lone parents were caring for others, mainly caring for elderly parents outside the household (Marsh *et al.* 2001).

Income and ethnic origin are interconnected factors in determining the experience of being a carer. The Caring on the Breadline survey found that 46 per cent of Black British/European carers and 42 per cent from other ethnic groups were, or had been, in debt, compared to 34 per cent of all carers. Black British/European carers were more likely to have given up work to provide care (67 per cent) than all carers (59 per cent), and Black British/European carers were more likely to find that benefits did not cover the cost of disability (67 per cent) compared with all carers (53 per cent) (Holzhausen and Pearlman 2000). Other earlier studies have suggested that interrelated factors such as income, class, health and housing impact on the diversity of carers. Compared to working-class families, middle-class people may have a longer list of viable alternatives to providing care themselves, such as paying for care (Arber and Ginn 1992a). So research consistently demonstrates that working-class families were more likely to care for someone other than their children and, importantly, were more likely to take the person they cared for into their own home.

CARERS OVER PENSION AGE

Ageism is rife in the literature on carers over pension age. The premise that the majority of care giving is to frail elderly relatives and that they, as a social group, are a growing burden to society has done little to stimulate awareness of the interdependence of active senior citizens in receiving and providing care. The research literature has colluded with media representations that older people are 'conceptualised as a passive object to be cared for' (Arber and Ginn 1992b, p.87). This neglects and ignores the evidence that only very small minorities of elderly people are disabled and need care. Many older people prefer to remain independent and outside care services (informal or formal) for as long as possible. 'Since the majority of physically frail elderly people are aware of how others see them, they are likely to internalise this perception of themselves as a burden, and as a source of strain to the carer' (p.97). Consequently, spouses over pension age provide most of the support with personal tasks, with only a tiny amount of care provided by professional services and by other kin carers (p.101).

Conclusion

In the research literature, carers have been generally described in three broad ways: in terms of attributes of themselves (young carers, rural carers), in terms of attributes of the cared-for person (carers of people with dementia) and in terms of their relationship (parent carers). In the conduct of public policy, the political acceptance of carers as a category in their own right and of caring as a generic activity has been credited with enabling significant service development for informal carers in the 1990s (Twigg and Atkin 1994) and early twenty-first century. Having created a base for generic carer services, current practice needs to engage with a range of client groups (users and the 'hidden' non-users) with cognisance of the key variables (age, class, disability, gender, income, mental health problems, 'race'/ethnicity, residence) that differentiate between carers and their unmet needs.

Notes

1. Source: derived from General Household Survey 1995, as in House of Commons, Hansard, 25 May 2000, col 589w, cited in Howard (2001).
2. Data from the Young Carers Research Group, Loughborough University.
3. Proposed in Department of Health, 'Valuing People: A New Strategy for Learning Disabilities for the 21st century'. White Paper, Cm 5086, March 2001.
4. Where one or both of the couple are working and earning up to the family credit level plus 35 per cent (but not higher than this).

References

Acheson, D. (1998) *Independent Inquiry into Inequalities in Health.* London: The Stationery Office.

Ahmad, W.I.U. (2000) *Ethnicity, Disability and Chronic Illness.* Buckingham: Open University Press.

Ahmad, W. and Atkin, K. (1996) *'Race' and Community Care.* Buckingham: Open University Press.

Aldridge, J. and Becker, S. (1993) *Children Who Care: Inside the World of Young Carers.* Loughborough: Loughborough University.

Aldridge, J. and Becker, S. (1996) 'Disability rights and the denial of young carers: the danger of zero-sum arguments.' *Critical Social Policy 16*, 55–76.

Arber, S. and Ginn, J. (1992a) 'Class and caring: a forgotten dimension.' *Sociology 26*, 619 634.

Arber, S. and Ginn, J. (1992b) 'In sickness and in health': care-giving, gender and the independence of elderly people.' In C. Marsh and S. Arber (eds) *Families and Households: Divisions and Change.* Basingstoke: Macmillan.

Beatty, C. and Fothergill, S. (1999) *The Detached Male Workforce.* Sheffield: Centre for Regional Economic and Social Research, Sheffield Hallam University.

Becker, S., Aldridge, J. and Dearden, C. (1998) *Young Carers and their Families.* London: Blackwell.

Beresford, B. (1995) *Expert Opinions: A National Survey of Parents Caring for a Severely Disabled Child.* Bristol: The Policy Press.

Brody, E.M. (1981) 'Women in the middle and family help to older people.' *The Gerontologist 21*, 471–480.

Chamba, R., Ahmad, W., Hirst, M., Lawton, D. and Beresford, B. (1999) *On the Edge: Minority Ethnic Families Caring for a Severely Disabled Child.* Bristol: Joseph Rowntree Foundation/The Policy Press.

Cree, V.E. (1996) 'Why do men care?' In K. Cavanagh and V.E. Cree (eds) *Working with Men: Feminism and Social Work.* London: Routledge.

Dearden, C. and Becker, S. (2001) *Growing up Caring: Vulnerability and Transition to Adulthood – Young Carers' Experiences.* Leicester: National Youth Agency/Joseph Rowntree Foundation.

Department of Health (1998) *Modernising Mental Health Services: Safe, Sound and Supportive.* London: Department of Health.

Department of Health (1999) *Caring about Carers: A National Strategy for Carers.* London: HM Government Department of Health. ttp://www.doh.gov.uk/carers.htm

Dobson, B., Middleton, S. and Beardsworth, A. (2001) *The Impact of Childhood Disability on Family Life.* York: Joseph Rowntree Foundation.

Eley, S. and Lee-Treweek, G. (2001) *Responding to Young Carers: The Rural Dimension.* Stirling: The Princess Royal Trust for Carers, Stirling Carers Centre.

Finch, J. and Groves, D. (eds) (1983) *A Labour of Love: Women, Work and Caring.* London: Routledge & Kegan Paul.

Finch, J. and Mason, J. (1993) *Negotiating Family Responsibilities.* London: Routledge.

Fisher, M. (1994) 'Man-made care: Community care and older male carers.' *British Journal of Social Work 24*, 659–680.

Fisher, M. (1997) 'Older male carers and community care.' In J. Bornat, J. Johnson, C. Pereira, D. Pilgrim and F. Williams (eds) *Community Care: A Reader* (2nd edn). Basingstoke: Macmillan and Open University.

Glendinning, C. (1992) *The Costs of Informal Care: Looking inside the Household.* London: HMSO.

Goodinge, S. (2000) *A Jigsaw of Services: Inspection of Services to Support Disabled Adults in their Parenting Role.* London: Social Services Inspectorate/Department of Health.

Graham, H. (1997) 'Feminist perspectives on caring.' In J. Bornat, J. Johnson, C. Pereira, D. Pilgrim and F. Williams (eds) *Community Care: A Reader* (2nd edn). Basingstoke: Macmillan and Open University.

Gunaratnam, Y. (1997) 'Breaking the silence: Black and ethnic minority carers and service provision.' In J. Bornat, J. Johnson, C. Pereira, D. Pilgrim and F. Williams (eds) *Community Care: A Reader* (2nd edn). Basingstoke: Macmillan and Open University.

Harvey, K. (2001) 'Being a carer.' In R. Ramsey, C. Gerada, S. Mars and G. Szmukler (eds) *Mental Illness: A Handbook for Carers.* London: Jessica Kingsley Publishers.

Heron, C. (1998) *Working with Carers.* London: Jessica Kingsley Publishers.

Hirst, M. (2001) 'Trends in informal care in Great Britain during the 1990s.' *Health and Social Care in the Community 9*, 6, 348–357.

Holzhausen, E. and Pearlman, V. (2000) *Caring on the Breadline: The Financial Implications of Caring.* London: Carers National Association.

Howard, M. (2001) *Paying the Price: Carers, Poverty and Social Exclusion.* London: Child Poverty Action Group in association with Carers UK.

Howe, G. (1999) *Mental Health Assessments.* London: Jessica Kingsley Publishers.

Lewis, J. and Meredith, B. (1988) *Daughters who Care Alone.* London: Routledge.

Marsh, A., McKay, S., Smith, A. and Stephenson, A. (2001) *Low-income Families in Britain: Work, Welfare and Social Security in 1999.* DSS Research Report 138. London: Corporate Document Services.

Mir, G., Nocon, A., Ahmad, W. and Jones, L. (2001) *Learning Difficulties and Ethnicity.* London: Department of Health.

Morris, J. (1991) *Pride against Prejudice: Transforming Attitudes to Disability.* London: Women's Press.

Morris, J. (1995) 'Creating a space for absent voices: Disabled women's experience of receiving assistance with daily living activities.' *Feminist Review 51*, 68–93.

Morris, J. (1997) 'A response to Aldridge and Becker – "Disability rights and the denial of young carers: The danger of zero-sum arguments"'. *Critical Social Policy 17*, 133–135.

Nazroo, J. (1997) *Ethnicity and Mental Health.* London: Policy Studies Institute.

Nissel, M. and Bonnerjea, L. (1982) *Family Care of the Handicapped Elderly: Who Pays?* London: Policy Studies Institute.

Olsen, R. (1996) 'Young carers: Challenging the facts and politics of research into children and caring.' *Disability and Society 11*, 1, 41–54.

Patel, N. (1990) *'Race' against Time: Social Services Provision to Black Elders.* London: Runnymede Trust.

Qureshi, H. and Walker, A. (1989) *The Caring Relationship.* Basingstoke: Macmillan.

Rowlands, O. and Parker, G. (1998) *Informal Carers: Results of an independent study carried out by the Office for National Statistics on behalf of the Department of Health as part of the 1995 General Household Survey.* London: Office for National Statistics.

Scottish Executive (1999) *Strategy for Carers in Scotland.* Edinburgh: Scottish Executive Health Department. http://www.scotland.gov.uk/library2/doc10/carerstrategy.asp

Shah, R. and Hatton, C. (1999) *Caring Alone: Young Carers in South Asian Communities.* London: Barnardo's.

Social Exclusion Unit. (2000) *Minority Ethnic Issues in Social Exclusion and Neighbourhood Renewal.* London: Cabinet Office.

Social Services Inspectorate (1999) *They Look After their Own Don't They?* London: Social Services Inspectorate.

Tester, S. (1996) 'Women and community care.' In C. Hallett (ed) *Women and Social Policy: An Introduction.* London: Harvester Wheatsheaf.

Thomas, C. (1993) 'De-constructing concepts of care.' *Sociology 27,* 4, 649–669.

Twigg, J. and Atkin, K. (1994) *Carers Perceived: Policy and Practice in Informal Care.* Buckingham: Open University Press.

Ward, C. (2001) *Family Matters: Counting Families In.* London: Department of Health.

Wates, M. (1997) *Disabled Parents: Dispelling the Myths.* Oxford: Radcliffe Medical Press in association with the National Childbirth Trust.

Wates, M. (2000) *Young Carers: Disabled Parents' Perspective.* Disabled Parents Network http://www.DisabledParentsNetwork.org.uk/

Williams, R., Eley, S., Hunt, K. and Bhatt, S. (1997) 'Has psychological distress among South Asians been underestimated? A comparison of three measures in the West of Scotland population.' *Journal of Ethnicity and Health 2,* 1/2, 21–29.

CHAPTER 4

Carers and Assessment

Hazel Qureshi, Hilary Arksey and Elinor Nicholas

Introduction

Assessment which takes place in a situation where a family carer is involved must incorporate some duality of focus, while at the same time seeking to reconcile agency agendas with those of the user and carer. A number of policy initiatives over the past ten years have sought to influence assessment practice with carers. Although policy as embodied in legislation has tended to emphasise the aim of sustaining and maintaining informal care, strategy documents and subsequent guidance have acknowledged the importance of enabling carers to draw boundaries around what they will do and to reduce involvement if this is what they wish, and of taking account of user preferences about sources of care. However, the pressure on budgets and the imperative to meet statutory obligations impose constraints on the freedom to support such choices (Hardy, Young and Wistow 1999; Richards 2000). The inherent tensions in policy itself, and variations in local implementation, have produced a context for practice which undoubtedly gives a greater prominence to carers but which conveys mixed messages to practitioners about the appropriate balances to be struck in producing an agreed package of services. Assessors have been criticised for focusing too much on carers' views rather than those of users (Davis, Ellis and Rummery 1997); for being user-centred and ignoring carers' needs (Seddon and Robinson 2001); and for not appreciating that conflict within families may well reflect inadequate state services for both users and carers rather than poor family functioning (Williams and Robinson 2001). At the same time, aspects of good practice in assessment, from a carer and user perspective, have been identified and observed. Striking an appropriate balance between carer and user views, and negotiating an agreed way forward, given agency, user and carer agendas, has been recognised as a key aspect of assessment practice (Baldwin 2000; Hardiker and Barker 1999; Smale *et al.* 1994).

This chapter will consider the national policy background to carer assessment, and research which considers the influence of policy changes on practice, as well as wider research which provides findings which might support practitioners in conducting assessment with carers.

Legislative/policy background

The community care reforms of the early 1990s were described as introducing a shift from a service-led to a needs-led approach to assessment. Assessment was said to be the 'cornerstone' of good quality community care (DoH 1990). However, research conducted in the wake of the new arrangements was critical of the assessment and care management process. For instance, assessment was seen as a means for managing demand rather than an opportunity to provide support (Ellis 1993). Surveys of carers who had been assessed showed reduced levels of satisfaction: many felt their own needs were not met. In efforts to improve support for carers and to ensure that the caring role was integrated within the new community care structures, a statutory right to assessment was advocated (Warner 1995).

The Carers (Recognition and Services) Act 1995 came into force in England, Wales and Scotland in April 1996. This was a step forward in acknowledging both the role that carers play in supporting disabled people and the needs which carers themselves have (SSI 1998). The Act gave carers who provided 'regular' and 'substantial' help the right to an assessment of their ability to care, and to continue caring, at the same time as the care recipient was being assessed for community care provision. Local authorities were required to take the results of the assessment into account when making decisions about services in respect of the care recipient.

The Carers Act (1995) was welcomed, particularly by carers' organisations, but areas of concern remained. Local government organisations and the Association of Directors of Social Services were concerned that the Act imposed a duty to assess without the power, or additional resources, to provide direct services to carers (Arksey, Hepworth and Qureshi 2000). The requirement to link carer assessment to the assessment of users' needs seemed unnecessarily restrictive. Concerns were expressed, for example, that the legislation had the potential to highlight tensions and conflicts of interest between service users and carers (Williams and Robinson 2000), and that resource constraints would continue to encourage a service-led approach in reality (Seddon 1999).

Studies of the implementation of the Act have found that, generally, local policy responses to the Carers Act reflected central policy intentions, although of course this does not prove a causal connection between the two. Managers and practitioners often argued that such changes were underway in any case (Arksey *et al.* 2000). However, some key aspects of implementation at a local level did not follow recommendations. There were clear gaps in relation to informing carers of their entitlement to assessment, discussing how the assessment should be conducted, confirming the results of the assessment in writing, and monitoring or reviewing carers' needs and circumstances. Research with carers showed that their knowledge of the legislation was minimal, that many carers were not aware at the time of the event that they were being assessed, that the arrangements for the assessment – including the question of a separate discussion not in the presence of the care recipient – were not always a matter for negotiation and agreement and that written follow-up and/or further review was often not provided (Arksey *et al.* 2000; CNA 1997a, 1997b; Seddon and Robinson 2001; SSI 1998; Williams and Robinson 2000).

In February 1999, the new Labour Government published *Caring about Carers: A National Strategy for Carers* (DoH 1999a) which acknowledged and responded to many of the research findings and criticisms from carers' organisations. The Assembly of Wales has since implemented its own strategy for carers (National Assembly for Wales 2000) and the Scottish Government has published a strategy for Scotland (Scottish Executive 1999). The national strategies exemplify 'joined-up' government in that they present policies cutting across traditional departmental boundaries and recognising the links to wider issues such as employment and pensions as well as health and social care.

The most recent government initiative is the new Carers and Disabled Children Act 2000, which came into effect in April 2001. This latest legislation, which applies in England and Wales only, strengthens the 1995 Carers Act by introducing a new right for a carer to receive an assessment, if they request it, even where the care recipient has refused an assessment for, or the provision of, community care services. In addition, authorities now have the power to provide direct services to carers to meet their needs. A complication introduced by giving authorities this new power is that carers can now be charged for services designed to assist and support them in their caring role – a situation regarded by carers' organisations as unjust, given that the need arises only because the carer is providing services which might otherwise be the responsibility of government. The documentation accompanying the new Act is comprehensive and includes a detailed practitioner's guide designed to be a good practice tool for staff carrying out carers' assessments (DoH 2001a). The latter guidance lists dimensions of carer assessment whose importance are well supported by research but, if past experience is repeated, frontline workers may never see the guidance, or may feel that, in a context of budget restrictions and the need to preserve adequate care arrangements for users, they are difficult to translate into practice (Seddon and Robinson 2001). As with the 1995 Act, no new resources have been attached to the legislation, although as part of the implementation of the National Carers Strategy, local authorities received some additional funds to develop services for carers. It is too early to know what impact the Carers and Disabled Children Act (2000) is having, although studies of the previous Act and its consequences may prove instructive. The remainder of this chapter will draw on research examining the reality of practice in the wake of the 1995 Act, as well as wider research findings which may provide support for improvements in policy and practice relating to carer assessment. Specifically, the chapter will address access to assessment, the process of assessment and the content of assessment.

Access to assessment

One particularly crucial area where local policy did not necessarily follow central government's intentions relates to those carers qualifying for an assessment. The terms 'regular' and 'substantial' were not defined in the 1995 Act, and the accompanying guidance (DoH 1996) suggested they should be interpreted 'in their everyday sense'. The practice guidance (SSI 1996) confirmed the emphasis on 'heavily involved' carers (Parker and Lawton 1994) rather than 'helpers' and detailed a number of factors indicative of whether someone was providing substantial and regular care: the type and intensity of care undertaken; the level of supervision involved; and whether caring was likely to be a continuing responsibility. Evidence suggests that rationing decisions in relation to carer assessment are often made on the basis of implicit assumptions about the level of physical care provided, and considerations about time or other resources available (Arksey 2002; Banks 1999; Nicholas 2003). An important issue for senior policy managers was to prioritise not only *among* carers but also *between* carers and care recipients. Since the right to an assessment was dependent upon the service user being assessed, so, by default, carers were ranked on the same basis adopted for users: urgency, risk and (in)dependence (Arksey 2002).

Reaching a definition of 'regular and substantial care' proved difficult for many local authorities, and evidence indicated that they developed a multitude of definitions of the terms (Arksey *et al.* 2000; CNA 1997b; Seddon and Robinson 2001). Consequently, eligibility for assessment varies both within and between authorities and some carers find it more difficult than others to access their right to be assessed. Studies of implementation suggest lower than expected take-up of new rights to carer assessment, and differential access for some groups of carers, for example older carers, and those from minority ethnic groups (Arksey *et al.* 2000; CNA 1997b; Khatbamna and Bhakta 1998; SSI 1998).

The reality facing practitioners is that there are insufficient resources to offer a comprehensive, or in-depth, assessment to all carers and, furthermore, not all carers will require or want one (Nicholas 2001; Nolan and Philp 1999). The questions of who should receive what type of assessment and how such judgements are informed are therefore matters of great significance. On initial contact it is important to discover and respond to the most pressing issues for the carer and to determine whether they may benefit from a comprehensive assessment. A European Union Funded

Project, COPE (Carers of Older People in Europe) aims to introduce a more distinct, three-stage approach to assessing carers which involves, identifying carers, an initial or first-stage assessment, and an in-depth assessment (Nolan and Philp 1999). Towards this end, the COPE Index includes 15 questions aiming to elicit carers' perceptions of both the positive and negative aspects of caring and existing support structures. The questions focus on the carers' view of their role; the demands and restrictions placed upon them; the extent of negative impact experienced (on relationships with family and friends, physical health and emotional well-being); how well they feel able to cope, their sense of recognition and value in care giving and the quality of their relationship with the person they care for. COPE has been tested across five European countries and found to be valid and reliable, with slight cultural variations, but apart from one successful study carried out in Poland, has yet to be widely tested for acceptability in routine practice (Mckee *et al.* 2001; Wojszel, Bien and Wilmanska 2001). Other studies in Canada, Australia and the UK have independently reached similar conclusions about the need for a staged approach to carer assessment and have developed, or are in the process of developing, various tools to support this process. For example, in Canada, one study has developed a Caregiver Risk Screen (alongside a comprehensive Caregiver Assessment Tool), to be used on initial contact to determine the level of risk to a carer's physical and/or mental well being with a view to establishing the urgency of inter-vention (Guberman *et al.* 2001). In Australia, another study is in the process of developing a 'Carer Screening Tool' that will be embedded in the care recipient's assessment, similarly aiming to identify the circumstances which 'put carers at risk of a reduction in their physical, mental and social well-being', but intended to target resource intensive comprehensive assessments to those most likely to benefit from an intervention (Rembicki 2001). In the UK, a further study, aiming to introduce an outcomes focus into carer assessment and review, developed an introductory or first-stage carer assessment tool. Influenced by the work of Nolan, Grant and Keady (1996), it aimed to elicit the carer's view of key strengths and difficulties in their situation as well as their aspirations, and to assist professional judgements about the need for a more in-depth assessment (Nicholas 2001, 2003). This tool, intended for self-completion where appropriate, was experienced by practitioners and carers as a helpful first step towards an informed discussion between carer and assessor about desired outcomes.

The process of assessment

What approach to carers' assessments was advocated for the Carers Act 1995? The practice aims and objectives included a range of key emphases: practitioners should not assume a willingness by the carer to continue caring; carers and professional staff should share the same understanding of the process; practitioners should discuss with the carer how the assessment should be done, adopt an integrated, family-based approach and confirm care plans and assessment results in writing (SSI 1996). The practice guide (SSI 1996) indicated that assessment would probably involve a face-to-face discussion, with an option that it took place in private and in that sense was 'separate'.

What makes a good assessment process from the user and carer viewpoint? In Davis, Ellis and Rummery (1997) positive assessment encounters, as defined by disabled people and carers, had the following features:

- provision of information about the purpose of assessment

- face-to-face encounters which focused on people's definitions of their main concerns

- the assessor valued them and their expertise.

Similarly, Arksey *et al.* (2000, p.37) identified in 'Carers' reflections on assessment practice' the following features of good practice in assessment drawing on views of 51 carers who had received an assessment under the 1995 Act:

- The assessment process is made explicit and carers are given time and information in preparation for the discussions.

- Consideration is given to the timing and arrangements for interviews, particularly when caring responsibilities or work commitments make it difficult to fit in with the office hours of social services staff.

- Carers are given the opportunity for an informed choice over the matter of privacy and 'separate' assessment.

- Carers have face-to-face discussion, with self-assessment and other forms being an aid to this process rather than an alternative.

- Care is taken with the amount of written information, which some carers find difficult to absorb even if they find time to read it.

- Workers are prompt in responding to the carer assessment and maintain contact, even when no further direct support services result from the assessment.

- Written confirmation of the result of the assessment is backed by some, albeit limited, direct contact follow-up as a support and safeguard.

It will be evident that much of the approach perceived as good practice in the process of assessment involves flexibility in fitting in with carer and user preferences. In that sense process and content of assessment are inextricably linked. Although some carers report benefit from the assessment itself, even if no services are provided, the process is usually expected to result in a care plan which will detail support and assistance to be provided, together with some statement of intended outcomes (DoH 2001a, 2001b, 2001c).

The knowledge for assessment

In a recent study of the attitudes of social services staff towards evidence-based practice, Sheldon and Chilvers (2000, p.75) found some scepticism about the concentration of much recent research on investigating policy-led structural change and a wish to know about research which could support effective practice. With regard to assessment, key messages from a range of recent studies have highlighted the importance of a broader appreciation of the nature and complexity of care giving and its impact on individuals (Nolan *et al.* 1996); developing more positive ways of perceiving carers and their relationship with the formal care sector (Guberman *et al.* 2001; Nolan *et al.* 1996; Twigg and Atkin 1994); greater clarity around the purpose of assessment and subsequent interventions, and understanding the type of outcomes carers value (Nolan and Philp 1999; Nicholas 2001).

Katbamna and Bhakta (1998) argued that workers too often stereotype people from minority ethnic groups by making incorrect assumptions about their likely access to informal care. However, at the same time, older people from minority ethnic groups have argued that many workers lack an understanding of family structures and family obligations in their community (Qureshi *et al.* 1998). This example illustrates the challenge for practice in using available knowledge and evidence whilst treating each individual case as unique.

The evidence base relevant to the content of assessment

Knowledge from research can support assessment and care planning practice in a number of ways. These are summarised in Box 4.1, and will be discussed in turn.

Box 4.1 How research can support individual practice in assessment

- Provide an understanding of the experience of caring, including sources of satisfaction.

- Identify services or ways of working which carers feel are of help to them.

- Identify common problems facing carers, particularly those known to be associated with care not being sustained or negative impacts on the carer or the service user.

- Provide evidence about ways of addressing problems or sustaining care.

Specifically research can support assessment by enabling practitioners to develop rapport and to show familiarity with the kinds of problems and satisfactions carers might identify and the outcomes they may be looking for; to be aware of key problems which, if not addressed, may lead to carer stress, or to care not being sustained; to identify a range of possible ways of addressing the problems, difficulties or desired outcomes identified in a particular situation.

UNDERSTANDING CARE GIVING AND RECEIVING

Research findings indicate both the diversity of experiences of caring relationships and the commmonalities. A developing understanding of care giving within the literature has emphasised the complex, dynamic nature of care giving which is interactive, contextual, temporal, based in relationships and an experience which changes over time (Nolan *et al.* 1996). It is essential that assessment and service responses are sensitive to the more sophisticated understanding of care giving which has emerged. This will include an appreciation of the carer's motivation and purposes in the caring role and the nature and sources of stress experienced. In addition, evidence suggests that satisfaction or reward can be an important component of the care giving experience, and where absent may give cause for considerable concern. Nolan *et al.* (1996) valuably point to the importance of a temporal perspective, arguing in depth that interventions have to be tailored to the stage of care giving history. National data indicates that effects on carers' emotional health increase as the length of time involved in caring increases, and this effect increases with the number of hours per week of involvement (Hutton and Hirst 2001). Most often carer assessment takes place after the commencement of caring, sometimes years after (Levin, Moriarty and Gorbach 1994). These findings support the importance of a temporal perspective on caring, thus understanding the kinds of assistance likely to be welcomed at different stages of caring activity (Nolan *et al.* 1996). Many carers, by the time they come into contact with services, will have developed a range of strategies for managing caring which can be easily undermined by services. A more rounded understanding of the specific difficulties, satisfactions and preferred coping strategies of individual carers is therefore likely to lead to more relevant and effective interventions (Nolan *et al.* 1996, 1998).

It is established in the carer literature that the relationship between objective measures, such as the level of impairment of the cared-for person or the kind and frequency of tasks performed, is less closely related to carers' perceptions of their own stress or strain than might have been supposed. One prominent response to this finding has been the development of work on styles of coping, where stress is conceptualised as a process through which the individual assesses potential stressors and brings to bear a variety of resources to deal with them (see, for example Beresford 1994; Sloper *et al.* 1991). Thus individual styles of coping are seen as mediating between external factors and a person's responses. This more positive model, of people actively constructing their own ways of living and dealing with difficulties, has underpinned some interventions designed to assist people 'at risk' to adjust their coping behaviours towards those which are more effective in their particular circumstances (Gammon and Rose 1991; Kirkham 1993). Work on stress and coping indicates that the relationship between different stressors and the way these are perceived and experienced will be unique to each individual carer (Aneshensel *et al.* 1995; Bowers 1987).

COMMON PROBLEMS

Although carers do cope differentially with apparently similar circumstances, none the less there are some consistent findings in the carer literature about the relationship between particular features of the caring situation and outcomes. These findings are valuable in indicating important dimensions for assessment of carers' needs as well as areas for outcome measurement. For example, the presence of severe behavioural difficulties on the part of the cared-for person has been widely demonstrated to influence both the carer's levels of distress and the eventual decision to seek alternatives to family care (Gilleard 1987; Gilleard *et al.* 1984; Levin, Sinclair and Gorbach 1989; Quine and Pahl 1985; Qureshi 1993). In general, difficult behaviour is more important in influencing these latter outcomes than, for example, levels of physical impairment of the cared-for person. There is an increasing recognition that practical tasks in themselves may be a relatively unimportant factor in the creation of distress, except when their performance imposes high opportunity costs or, for example, involves loss of sleep.

Key factors commonly identified as important in relation to distress or admission to a residential service include:

- behaviour by the person cared for which is difficult to manage or accept – especially if this involves self-injury, dangerous behaviour (intended or not), violence which cannot be controlled, frequent lack of co-operation in care or socially unacceptable behaviour in public

- lack of sleep for the carer

- continuous unremitting need for supervision or physical tending – for older people, severe cognitive impairment is more likely than physical impairment to be associated with eventual admission to a residential service

- opportunity costs – for example, the demands of caring prevent social life or employment

- poor physical health of carer

- poor mental health of carer

- quality of the relationship (findings are complex, given the variety of relationships (e.g. parent/child; adult child/parent; spouses) but past and present quality as perceived by the carer is associated with willingness to continue, as well as carer mental health).

In addition, it is helpful to note that, for older people at least, relatives' expressed willingness to accept residential care is a far better predictor of eventual placement in such care than many other factors, including levels of distress (Askham and Thompson 1990; Levin, Moriarty and Gorbach 1994; Levin, Sinclair and Gorbach 1989). The evidence for the identification of key problems comes from both cross-sectional and longitudinal studies conducted through the last twenty years, and involving a range of user groups. There are a number of reservations about translating this research into a basis for practice. First, it has sometimes implicitly defined the move to alternatives to family care as a 'bad thing', whereas this is clearly not always so. Admission to a residential service for an older person can be an appropriate response to circumstances and individual preferences. Parents of adults with learning disability may seek alternatives to family care because they believe this is consistent with ideas about independence and a normal life, and not as a consequence of their own distress. The disability movement, in seeking to promote user empowerment and social justice, has argued that the focus on carer stress distracts attention from the rights of service users because in fact carers need services only because service users' rights to independent living are not upheld (Morris 1997). This clash of perspectives has been evident in debates over young carers, where disabled people have argued that the problems and needs for assistance of school-age children caring for parents reflect a failure by the state to support disabled people in their parenting role. (See Becker, Dearden and Aldridge 2000 for a general review of this topic.) Other researchers have similarly argued that apparent conflict between family members and carers may result from common interest in improved services from the state (Qureshi and Walker 1989; Williams and Robinson 2000).

A second concern is that the range of outcomes of importance has been too limited. It has been argued that ordinary life goals (for example, to work or not, to enjoy a social life), choice and independence are as valid for carers as they are for users of services (Nocon and Qureshi 1996), and that services which can achieve these outcomes are therefore to be valued whether or not they lead to reduced stress or continued care. Finally, there is a wariness about the danger of a mechanistic translation of such findings into a 'tick-box' approach to assessment which ignores the variety of individual experience, aspirations and preferences which inevitably confront the practitioner in their day-to-day work with disabled people and families. This is an important concern, and a research-based approach which attempts to support a more holistic way of working will be discussed later. However, these findings about common problems do have implications for practice because this body of research suggests that services, or individual interventions, which tackle these issues might be useful in reducing stress, or extending the length of care giving, and that a repertoire of possible responses for dealing with such problems would be a useful resource for a practitioner to call on in individual cases. It does not, of course, predetermine an appropriate response in any individual situation. As an example, not getting enough sleep might be a consequence of the person cared for being awake much of the night because of inadequately controlled pain, or it might be a consequence of behavioural difficulties shown by a young child with learning difficulties, or wakefulness and wandering on the part of a person with dementia. There are many other possibilities. If the carer wanted services to aim towards an outcome of increased sleep then ways to achieve that outcome might therefore include better pain relief for the user, behavioural interventions, night sitting services, or overnight care elsewhere. Good practice must involve combining existing knowledge with analysis and investigation of the individual situation.

EFFECTIVENESS OF INTERVENTIONS AND SERVICES

Much of the UK evidence is from carers' accounts of services, indicating things which they did or did not find helpful and services which carers would like. Thus it is known that in general they like to have easy access to services (good information, a named contact, back-up help in emergencies, for example) and there is an understanding of the outcomes they look for in broad terms – good quality of life for the person cared for, their own separate quality of life, and practical and emotional support in the caring role. They often identify unmet needs for information, breaks or respite, emotional support and financial advice (Arksey *et al.* 2000; Banks 1999; Kersten *et al.* 2001; Nicholas 2001; Pickard 1999; Seddon and Robinson 2001).

Evidence which would prove scientifically the relationship between given services, however, or ways of intervening and particular outcomes is harder to find (Fortinsky 2001). There are some good reasons for the scarcity of evidence, not just the reluctance to fund such work: relationships between service inputs and outcomes are not so consistent as they often are in health (for example, respite care can help people cope for longer – although the evidence for this is weak, in fact – or it can act as a bridge to a situation where a carer gives up - this may sometimes be desirable). Exceptions to this scarcity of intervention studies are work on the effectiveness of behavioural interventions designed to tackle sleep problems (see, for example, Howcroft and Jones 1999; Quine 1993) and work, outside the UK, on helping carers to improve coping skills and problem solving approaches. For reviews of 'what works' in work with parents of disabled children, see Beresford *et al.*

(1999), and with carers of people with dementia, Cooke *et al.* (2001) and Pusey and Richards (2001). These reviews consistently conclude that only behaviour management and approaches designed to address problem solving and coping skills have demonstrated effectiveness. It is also clear that many intervention studies have poor methodology, and the range of definitions of what is meant by some interventions is so variable that results often cannot be compared across studies.

Where the evidence looks at the effects of services in a comparative way, the findings are usually that it is combinations of services (for example, home care and respite) and flexibility of delivery (helping out of normal working hours as well as during them, for example, or intensive care management) which produce the clearest observable effects (usually on carer stress, measured by psychosomatic symptom checklists) or on length of time an older person remains in the community (Davies and Fernandez 1999; Levin *et al.* 1989, 1994; Moriarty and Webb 2000). These findings illustrate that it is not so much what services that counts (although insufficient quantity is bad news) but whether they are delivered in a way which enables people to achieve the things that are important to them in reducing stress, improving satisfaction, making good opportunity costs and helping them to cope. Again this points to the importance of individual tailoring of support around the outcomes which carers identify as important.

Individual tailoring of assessment

PARTNERSHIP WITH CARERS

Nolan *et al.* (1996) point out that, currently, service interventions can range on a spectrum from the facilitative to the obstructive; the former engaging the carer as active partners, aiming to facilitate the best possible outcome for carer and cared for; the latter often inadvertently failing to appreciate the carer's goals or strategies in care giving and thereby creating more stress or guilt for the carer in accepting help. They suggest that a more explicit partnership with carers is required, aiming to recognise, promote and sustain a carer's expertise throughout the various stages of care giving. Seeing the carer as expert in this way would reinforce a facilitative approach towards carers and is consonant with an 'Exchange' model of assessment as described by Smale, Tuson, Biehal and Marsh (1993). Smale *et al.* defined three models: the Questioning, Procedural and Exchange models of assessment. In the Questioning or Procedural model the professional is expert in identifying the needs and appropriate responses according to certain criteria, focusing on dependencies and problems rather than strengths and possibilities in any situation. In contrast, the Exchange model of assessment acknowledges the differing contributions of user, carer and professional with the latter bringing 'expertise in the process of problem solving; the ability to work towards a mutual understanding of "the problem" with all the major actors' (Smale *et al.* 1993, p.16). Such an approach, which is supported by others (Guberman and Maheu 2002), would be sensitive to the carer's limits, seek to reduce difficulties but also build on strengths and enhance the carer's well-being in a more balanced way alongside that of the cared for person.

The purposes of the carer's assessment, identified in the Department of Health guidance to practitioners in 2001, are to determine the carer's eligibility for support, the type of support needed (to help them in their caring role and help them maintain their own health and well-being) and to see if those needs can be met by social or other services (DoH 2001a). Integral to these purposes are some new emphases, including consideration of the impact of caring and not just the time involved, and a carer-centred approach which focuses on 'the outcomes the carer would want to see' (DoH 2001a, para 29) within the context of a holistic assessment which recognises the interests of user and carer. The guidance emphasises, and good practice would indicate, that carer assessment should not be overly bureaucratic. It has been argued that sensitive user/carer centred assessments can be compromised by a requirement to complete inappropriate forms, and researchers have called for a more skilled and reflective approach (Moriarty and Webb, 2000). The guidance also emphasises the importance of focusing on what the carer wants to happen. Eighteen dimensions are outlined which might be relevant to explore with carers. While a flexible, skilled and carer-centred approach is key, the use of research-based assessment tools can facilitate a systematic approach which can enhance both practitioners' and carers' own understanding of the latter's needs, highlight carers' desired outcomes and lead to more effective care planning (Guberman *et al.* 2001; Nicholas 2001).

OUTCOMES

Identifying and agreeing intended outcomes with carers is an important dimension of assessment (DoH 2001a, 2001b, 2001c; Nicholas 2001). Based on the traditional concepts of caring, assessment of carers has been inclined to be problem oriented, with interventions geared to relieving distress or perceived strain, or preventing 'breakdown in caring relationships' assumed to be the result of intolerable pressures. We have suggested that such outcome 'measures' and interventions to achieve them are too general and that 'success' needs to be defined in a more individualistic manner by the carer herself in terms of what works for her. As a result of focus group discussions with carers, Nicholas (2001) specifies four distinct, but related, general dimensions of outcome which emerged as significant. These were:

1. *Quality of life for the person they support:* such as maintaining independence, personal cleanliness, comfort, dignity, safety and security, social contact and meaningful activity.

2. *Quality of life for the carer:* including physical and mental health and well-being, a sense of control over their life and caring role, positive relationships, peace of mind, financial security and freedom to maintain paid employment, social life, interests and other commitments alongside their caring responsibilities.

3. *Managing the caring role:* involving feeling informed, prepared, equipped and, where appropriate, trained for the caring task, a sense of shared responsibility, and being practically and emotionally supported.

4. *Service process outcomes:* referring to the impact of the way in which services are organised and delivered (for example, not giving carers a say in how a service is provided can ultimately affect morale and reduce their sense of control).

Following the development of this framework, an outcome-focused approach to carer assessment was developed and implemented on a trial basis in partnership with one local authority. This involved carers, practitioners and managers in developing and testing tools for carer assessment and review which aimed to promote an outcome focus in practice. The findings indicated that a clear conceptual framework and tools based on carers' views of valued outcomes could be useful in focusing assessments on what was most important to carers. According to practitioners, in some instances this led to care plans which were more specific and relevant to the individuals concerned than was usual. A range of assessment tools proved helpful in this study in enabling exploration with individual carers about their desired outcomes at differing levels of detail. These tools included various self-completion questionnaires used flexibly to facilitate an informed discussion with carers and a summary sheet to assist practitioners in the analysis and recording of outcomes information with a view to aggregation. Among the questionnaires tested for this purpose were the Carers' Indices (Nolan *et al.* 1996) which are three research-based instruments, each with up to 36 statements written from the carer's perspective to elicit a more in-depth profile of their perceived difficulties, satisfactions and management strategies. The benefits of this outcome-focused approach need to be balanced with a realistic appreciation of what is involved, including the time required for effective listening to carers, and training and support for staff in managing a significant cultural shift through a planned process of change (Nicholas 2001 and 2003; Qureshi 2001).

Conclusion

We have considered carer assessment in context, looking at specific research evidence about the impact of national and local policy changes and the actions of assessors, as well as wider evidence which might support practice. What were the main results of implementing the 1995 Carers Act? On a positive note, the legislation has been a motivator for change; it has led to improvements in local authorities' procedures, policies and support for carers, although in some instances these might have been going to happen anyway. The Act does seem to have helped some carers, especially those heavily involved: in the majority of cases where existing carers have been reassessed, services have been increased. At the same time, implementation has been piecemeal and its impact patchy, practice remains inconsistent, and joint working between health and social services is proving challenging. Despite some critical studies (Henwood 1998) the introduction of a more sensitive focus on carers in the work of the NHS has barely begun. Overall, it is evident that although policy on carers has become better developed, practice has yet to match stated policy aspirations. It remains to be seen whether the National Strategies for Carers are able to deliver the intended changes.

Research has offered some guidelines for the kind of approaches to assessment which may be valued by users and carers, even within this problematic context. It has also deepened our understanding of the experience of caring and pointed to key difficulties, desired outcomes from social services, sources of satisfaction and coping strategies. There is some evidence about the effectiveness of services and interventions, but although this evidence base needs to be improved it should not be expected that it will determine action in individual cases. Despite the identification of some common problems, diversity in the population of carers should not be understated. People caring for their spouses, their children, their neighbours or their parents have quite different experiences and needs. Different cultural and religious backgrounds are associated with different preferences and resources. We need to understand more about these differences as well as commonalities.

Caring takes place within a relationship, which will have its own unique history and established ways of behaving. Over time, the balance of care giving and receiving in a relationship may change, perhaps several times. Even at one point in time, there may not be a hard and fast distinction between carer and cared-for person. By no means all carers will want or need assistance, or welcome assessment. Others who might benefit will not ask, and decisions to offer assessment will thereby remain in the hands of professionals. Carer assessment will continue to involve taking account of user and carer agendas, within the constraints imposed by central policy and local policy and practice. New developments, such as the Social Care Institute for Excellence, intended to support evidence-based practice, may mean that care managers and social workers will have better access to research findings and potential new models to support good practice in screening for eligibility, partnership with carers, and an outcome focus in assessment and care planning. Equally, at the front line, research knowledge should support, rather than replace, professional judgement based on careful investigation and analysis of individual situations in partnership with service users and carers.

Acknowledgements

The Social Policy Research Unit receives support from the Department of Health. The views expressed in this chapter are those of the authors, and not necessarily those of the Department of Health.

References

Aneshensel, C.S., Pearlin, L.I., Mullan, J.T., Zarit, S.H. and Whitlatch, C.J. (1995) *Profiles in Caregiving: The Unexpected Career.* London: Academic Press Inc.

Arksey, H. (2002) 'Rationed care: Assessing the support needs of informal carers in English Social Services Authorities.' *Journal of Social Policy 31*, 1, 81–101.

Arksey, H., Hepworth, D. and Qureshi, H. (2000) *Carers' Needs and the Carers Act: An Evaluation of the Process and Outcomes of Assessment.* York: Social Policy Research Unit, University of York.

Askham, J. and Thompson, C. (1990) 'Dementia and Home Care.' Age Concern Research Paper No.4. Mitcham: Age Concern (England).

Baldwin, M. (2000) *Care Management and Community Care. Social Work Discretion and the Construction of Policy.* Aldershot: Ashgate Publishing Ltd.

Banks, P. (1999) *Carer Support: Time for a Change of Direction.* London: Kings Fund.

Becker, S., Dearden, C. and Aldridge, Jo. (2000) 'Young Carers in the UK: Research, Policy and Practice.' *Research, Policy and Planning 18*, 2, 13–21.

Beresford, B. (1994) 'Resources and strategies: How parents cope with the care of a disabled child.' *Journal of Child Psychology and Psychiatry 35*, 171–209.

Beresford, B., Sloper, P., Baldwin, S. and Newman, T. (1999) *What Works in Services for Families with a Disabled Child?* Barkingside: Barnardos.

Bowers, B.J. (1987) 'Inter-generational care giving: Adult caregivers and their ageing parents.' *Advances in Nursing Science 9*, 2, 2031.

CNA (Carers National Association) (1997a) *Still Battling? The Carers Act One Year On.* London: Carers National Association (now Carers UK).

CNA (Carers National Association) (1997b) *In on the Act: Social Services Experience of the First Year of the Carers Act.* London: Carers National Association.

Cooke, D., McNally, L., Mulligan, K., Harrison, M. and Newman, S. (2001) 'Psychosocial interventions for caregivers of people with dementia: A systematic review.' *Ageing and Mental Health 5*, 2, 120–135.

Davies, B. and Fernandez, J. with Nomer, B. (1999) *Equity and Efficiency Policy in Community Care.* Aldershot: Ashgate.

Davis, A., Ellis, K. and Rummery, K. (1997) *Access to Assessment: Perspectives of Practioners, Disabled People and Carers.* Bristol: Policy Press.

DoH (Department of Health) (1990) *Community Care in the Next Decade and Beyond.* London: HMSO.

DoH (Department of Health) (1996) *Carers (Recognition and Services) Act 1995: Policy Guidance.* London: Department of Health.

DoH (Department of Health) (1999) *Caring about Carers: A National Strategy for Carers.* London: Department of Health.

DoH (Department of Health) (2001a) *A Practitioner's Guide to Assessment under the Carers and Disabled Children Act 2000.* London: Department of Health.

DoH (Department of Health) (2001b) *Fair Access to Care Services: Policy Guidance Consultation Draft, July 2001.* London: Department of Health.

DoH (Department of Health) (2001c) *The Single Assessment Process: Guidance for Local Implementation, Consultation Draft, Annexes.* London: Department of Health.

Ellis, K. (1993) *Squaring the Circle: User and Carer Participation in Needs Assessment.* York: Joseph Rowntree Foundation.

Fortinsky, R. (2001) 'Health care triads and dementia care: Integrative framework and future directions.' *Ageing and Mental Health 5*, 2, (Supplement) 35–48.

Gammon, E. and Rose, S. (1991) 'The coping skills training program for parents of children with developmental disabilities: an experimental evaluation.' *Research on Social Work Practice 1*, 244–256.

Gilleard, C. (1987) 'Influence of emotional distress among supporters on the outcome of psychogeriatric day care.' *British Journal of Psychiatry 150*, 219–223.

Gilleard, C., Belford, H., Gilleard, J., Whittick, J. and Gledhill, K. (1984) 'Emotional distress amongst the supporters of the elderly mentally infirm'. *British Journal of Psychiatry 145*, 172–177.

Guberman, N., Keefe, J., Fancey, P., Nahmiash, D. and BaryLak, L. (2001) *Development of Screening and Assessment Tools for Family Caregivers.* NA 145 Montreal: School of Social Work, Université du Québec à Montréal.

Guberman, N. and Maheu, P. (2002) 'Conceptions of family care-givers: Implications for professional practice.' *Canadian Journal of Ageing 21*, 1, 25–35.

Hardiker, P. and Barker, M. (1999) 'Early steps in implementing the new community care: The role of social work practice.' *Health and Social Care in the Community 7*, 6, 414–426.

Hardy, B., Young, R. and Wistow, G. (1999) 'Dimensions of choice in the assessment and care management process: the views of older people, carers and care managers.' *Health and Social Care in the Community 7*, 6, 483–491.

Henwood, M. (1998) *Ignored and Invisible? Carers' Experience of the NHS.* London: Carers National Association.

Howcroft, D. and Jones, R. (1999) 'Sleep, older people and dementia.' *Nursing Times 18*, 8, 54–56.

Hutton, S. and Hirst, M. (2001) 'Informal care over time.' Research Works, August 2001. York: Social Policy Research Unit, University of York. Web: http://www.york.ac.uk/inst/spru/pubs.

Katbamna, S. and Bhakta, P. (1998) *Experiences and Needs of Carers from the South Asian Communities.* University of Leicester: Nuffield Community Care Studies Unit.

Kersten, P., McLellan, L., George, S., Mullee, M. and Smith, J. (2001) 'Needs of carers of severely disabled people: Are they identified and met adequately?' *Health and Social Care in the Community 9*, 4, 235–243.

Kirkham, M. (1993) 'Two year follow-up of skills training with mothers of children with disabilities.' *American Journal on Mental Retardation 97*, 509–520.

Levin, E., Moriarty, J. and Gorbach, P. (1994) *Better for the Break.* London: HMSO.

Levin, E., Sinclair, I. and Gorbach, P. (1989) *Families, Services and Confusion in Old Age.* Aldershot: Gower.

McKee, K., Philp, I., Nolan, M., Lamura, G., Spazzafumo, L., Prouskas, C., Öberg, B., Krevers, B. and Bien, B. (2001). 'The COPE index: An innovative instrument for first stage assessment of needs in informal carers.' *Gerontology 47*, Suppl 1, 223.

Moriarty, J. and Webb, S. (2000) *Part of Their Lives: Community Care for Older People with Dementia.* Bristol: Policy Press.

Morris, J. (1997) 'Care or empowerment? A disability rights perspective.' *Social Policy and Administration 31*, 54–60.

National Assembly for Wales (2000) *Caring about Carers: A Strategy for Carers in Wales.* Implementation Plan. Cardiff: National Assembly for Wales.

Nicholas, E. (2001) 'Implementing an outcome focus in carer assessment and review.' In H. Qureshi (ed) *Outcomes in Social Care Practice.* Outcomes in Community Care Practice Series No. 7, University of York: Social Policy Research Unit.

Nicholas, E. (2003) 'An outcomes focus in carer assessment and review: Value and challenge.' *British Journal of Social Work 33*, 1 (in press).

Nocon, A. and Qureshi, H. (1996) *Outcomes of Community Care for Users and Carers.* Buckingham: Open University Press.

Nolan, M., Grant, G. and Keady, J. (1996) *Understanding Family Care: A Multidimensional Model of Caring and Coping.* Buckingham: Open University Press.

Nolan, M., Grant, G. and Keady, J. (1998) *Assessing the Needs of Family Carers: A Guide for Practitioners.* Brighton: Pavilion Publishing.

Nolan, M. and Philp, I. (1999) 'COPE: Towards a comprehensive assessment of caregiver need.' *British Journal of Nursing 8*, 20, 18 November, 1364–1372.

Parker, G. and Lawton, D. (1994) *Different Types of Care, Different Types of Carer: Evidence from the General Household Survey.* London: HMSO.

Pickard, L. (1999) 'Policy options for informal carers of elderly people.' In *With Respect to Old Age Report* by the Royal Commission on Long Term Care, Cm 4192–II/3, Research vol. 3, Part 2, 1–98.

Pusey, H. and Richards, D. (2001) 'A systematic review of the effectiveness of psychosocial interventions for carers of people with dementia.' *Ageing and Mental Health 5*, 2, 107–119.

Quine, L. (1993) 'Working with parents: The management of sleep disturbance in children with learning disabilities.' In C. Kiernan (ed) *Research into Practice? Implications of Research on the Challenging Behaviour of People with Learning Disability.* Clevedon, Avon: BILD Publications.

Quine, L. and Pahl, J. (1985) 'Examining the causes of stress in families with severely mentally handicapped children.' *British Journal of Social Work 51*, 510–517.

Qureshi, H. (1993) 'Impact on Families.' In C. Kiernan (ed) *Research into Practice: Learning Disabilities and Challenging Behaviour.* Clevedon, Avon: British Institute of Learning Disability.

Qureshi, H. (ed) (2001) *Outcomes in Social Care Practice.* Outcomes in Community Care Practice Series no.7. University of York: Social Policy Research Unit.

Qureshi, H., Patmore, C., Nicholas, E. and Bamford, C. (1998) *Overview of Outcomes of Social Care for Older People and Carers.* Outcomes in Community Care Practice Series no.5. University of York: Social Policy Research Unit.

Qureshi, H. and Walker, A. (1989) *The Caring Relationship.* Basingstoke: Macmillan.

Rembicki, D. (2001) 'The Need/Rationale for Caregiver Assessment in Case Management.' Paper presented at symposium Assessing Caregivers: International Evaluations of Caregiver Assessment Tools and Assessment Experiences at 5th International Care/Case Management Conference, American Society on Ageing, Vancouver.

Richards, S. (2000) 'Bridging the divide: Elders and the assessment process.' *British Journal of Social Work 30*, 37–49.

Scottish Executive (1999) *Strategy for Carers in Scotland.* Edinburgh: Scottish Executive Health Department.

Seddon, D. (1999) *Carers of Elderly People with Dementia: Assessment and the Carers Act.* University of Wales, Bangor: Centre for Social Policy Research and Development.

Seddon, D. and Robinson, C.A. (2001) 'Carers of older people with dementia: Assessment and the Carers Act.' *Health and Social Care in the Community 9*, 3, 151–158.

Sheldon, B. and Chilvers, R. (2000) *Evidence-based Social Care: A Study of Prospects and Problems.* Lyme Regis: Russell House Publishing.

Sloper, P., Knussen, C., Turner, S. and Cunningham, C. (1991) 'Factors related to stress and satisfaction with life in families of children with Down's Syndrome.' *Journal of Child Psychology and Psychiatry 32*, 4, 655–676.

Smale, G., Tuson, G., Ahmad, B., Darvill, G., Domoney, L. and Sainsbury, E. (1994) *Negotiating Care in the Community*. London: HMSO.

Smale, G., Tuson, G., Biehal, N. and Marsh, P. (1993) *Empowerment, Assessment, Care Management and the Skilled Worker*. National Institute for Social Work Practice and Development Exchange. London: HMSO.

SSI (Social Services Inspectorate) (1998) *A Matter of Chance for Carers? Inspection of Local Authority Support for Carers*. London: Department of Health.

SSI (Social Services Inspectorate) (1996) *Carers (Recognition and Services) Act 1995: Practice Guide*. London: Department of Health.

Twigg, J. and Atkin, K. (1994) *Carers Perceived: Policy and Practice in Informal Care*. Buckingham: Open University Press.

Warner, N. (1995) *Better Tomorrows? Report of a National Study of Carers and the Community Care Changes*. London: Carers National Association.

Williams, V. and Robinson, C. (2000) *In Their Own Right: The Carers Act and Carers of People with Learning Disabilities*. Bristol: Policy Press.

Williams, V. and Robinson, C. (2001) 'More than one wavelength: Understanding and resolving conflicts of interest between people with intellectual difficulties and their family carers.' *Journal of Applied Research in Intellectual Disabilities 14*, 1, 30–46.

Wojszel, Z.B., Bien, B. and Wilmanska, J. (2001). 'Acceptability of the COPE Index in practitioners and carers of older people.' *Gerontology 47*, suppl. 1, 34.

CHAPTER 5

Caring Families

Their Support or Empowerment?

Gordon Grant

Introduction

This chapter seeks to argue a case for the development of a constellation of principles and practices, promulgated by services and rooted in families' beliefs and concerns, that families with disabled relatives can experience as empowering. Empowerment may still be regarded as a contested term (Case 2000; Murray 2000; Ramcharan *et al.* 1997; Twigg 2000) yet it implies that something beyond merely supporting people needs to happen if they are to be freed from experiencing marginalisation and oppression, and enabled to lead enriched and valued lives. In the case of family carers it will be argued that 'empowerment practice' has a number of predicates: the existence of salutogenic perspectives within family narratives about everyday care giving, the ability of families to articulate means and ends within their care giving, the scope of resilience and expertise within families, the mounting evidence about what helps families, and the development of thinking about the meaning of empowerment as opposed merely to support of families by formal agencies and other communities of interest. This is based largely on a reading of literature about families with disabled children, though it is felt that the underlying arguments have an application to other groups of families too. To begin with, an attempt is made to weigh some of the evidence about why current practice in supporting families needs to change.

Recognition without support

Families have long been the bedrock of care in or by the community, and this applies equally well to families of disabled children and adults. Indeed, the Prime Minister, Tony Blair, in launching the Carers National Strategy (DoH 1999), referred to family carers as the 'unsung heroes' essential to the fabric and character of Britain. Recognition indeed, but what hitherto has been the experience of families?

Some years ago Twigg and Atkin (1994) cogently argued that family carers occupied a rather ambiguous role relationship to services and professionals with four tacit models emergent. Viewed as resources by services, families would be maintained in their role as carers; viewed as co-workers they would attract greater recognition of their role from services; viewed as co-clients their needs are likely to be difficult to discriminate from those of the user; and, finally, in the case of the superseded carer, services would aim to replace or substitute them. From accounts of how services strive to support family care giving efforts (for example Knox *et al.* 2000; Nolan *et al.* 1996; Twigg and Atkin 1994; Williams and Robinson 2001a), it is apparent that services typically make the assumption that families are continuing to care (well) unless an alarm is raised. Within this scenario families would typically be perceived as resources, and therefore left for the most part to fend for themselves. Even with the Carers (Recognition and Services) Act 1995, which strove to give a particular category of family carers a right to an independent assessment of their needs, fundamental dimensions of the lives of families have been overlooked during professional assessment procedures (Robinson and Williams 1999).

Conceptualisations brought by academics and researchers to how families 'do their caring' have not helped very much and have been largely responsible for the perpetuation of a pathogenic view of families. Reviewing literature over twenty years on the adjustment of families rearing children with intellectual disabilities, for example, Helff and Glidden (1998) noted that though there had been some reduction in the use of negative language about families there was little evidence that researchers were reporting the achievements of family care any more. Most investigators still adopted language focusing on family difficulties and sources of stress. Concomitantly we find many services modelled primarily on assumptions about alleviating stress in families or providing them with a break from the 'daily grind' of caring. It is worth mentioning that within the huge body of literature on stress (and coping) in families, the views and perspectives of the disabled child or adult have been conspicuously absent.

Relationships between services and families can be further compounded by life-course factors. For example, families with babies, or young children with intellectual disabilities are more likely to be viewed as resources or even co-workers, with families benefiting from counselling, information, home support, family-based respite and specialist assessment and treatment of their child. However, as the child grows into adulthood the focus of professional attention, rightly or wrongly, is much more on the disabled adult rather than the family, with the range and intensity of support from formal services declining in tandem (McGrath and Grant 1993). Whether this planned or unintended withdrawal of services over the life course leads to heightened interdependence between older families and disabled adults who still live at home (Heller *et al.* 1997; Williams and Robinson 2001b) remains open to empirical study.

This raises a fundamentally important point, especially in the case of families who have children with lifelong cognitive or neurological problems that severely impair their capacity for self-expression. Taking the case of people with intellectual disabilities, Simpson (2001), for example, argues that there is a major difficulty with 'programming adulthood'. He suggests that research programmes and services have been influenced unduly by developmental psychology and theories about adaptation, and that self-determination, collective identity and political consciousness have been downplayed. So, for example, we might ask 'how do people with intellectual disabilities construe meaning and identity in their adult lives?' as the basis for developing a more informed idea of what they wish to do and how they might wish to develop their relationships with their families, services and the community at large, instead of assuming that activity, engagement, adaptation and quality of life are the necessary keys for shaping their support.

Adulthood also connotes capacity and autonomy, and with these come rights to confidentiality and privacy. This can of course lead to tensions between disabled adults and their families, especially in light of moves towards involving people, families and their disabled children or relatives as partners in support programmes. Pejlert (2001) provides a good example in the case of parents with sons or daughters with a mental illness.

Despite the best efforts of successive governments to sharpen the focus of family support services, many gaps in these services remain (Felce *et al.* 1998; Male 1998) in relation to coverage and accessibility, more of which is said later. This appears to be an international problem (Ashworth and Baker 2000; Pejlert 2001; Warfield and Hauser-Cram 1996). In short, it could be concluded that whilst services recognise the existence of families they are still struggling to support them.

Support without recognition?

The difficulties of making family support services stretch to reach families in more meaningful ways, implying better targeting, suggests also that too little is being done to recognise, respect and reinforce the many ways that families go about supporting their disabled children or adult relatives. Hence we find evidence of families complaining that their needs and circumstances are not understood, that professionals are failing to empathise with them, that many families are struggling to balance care and employment, that important cultural practices and traditions central to care giving are not being respected or that the role and contribution of different family members have been neither fully appreciated nor reinforced (Grant and Ramcharan 2001; Hatton *et al.* 1998; Jones *et al.* 2001; Knox *et al.* 2000; Shearn and Todd 2000). Even when their views are sought, carers frequently report that they are not listened to and that their contribution is only rarely acted upon (Henwood 1998; Warner and Wexler 1998).

It has been suggested that support directed towards families tends to be based on an understanding of family care giving as largely task-based rather than something that requires a lot of invisible work with cognitive and managerial dimensions (Nolan *et al.* 1996). The implication is that this de-limiting of professional orientation marginalizes important family care-giving activity, fails to capture its relevance to maintaining the dignity of the disabled child or relative, and too easily leads to the precluding of possibilities for partnership working. This is developed further in the section about the scope of resilience in families.

An inattention to the temporal aspects of family care giving by professionals is reported to leave carers feeling that little attention has been paid to periods of important decision making over the life course, especially in regard to how care giving was first taken up or how care giving responsibilities may need to be abrogated or relinquished in the best interests of their disabled child or adult relative (Bigby 1997; Grant 1990; Nolan *et al.* 1996; Prosser 1997). The sharing of care between family and formal services, whether this be 'respite/shared' care in all its forms or even the movement of the disabled relative into a separate, permanent living environment, raises important questions about the sharing of knowledge, cultural practices and care giving standards commensurate with maintaining a consistency in standards of support for the disabled child or adult across the informal and formal care sectors (Stalker 1990; Cotterill et al. 1997).

This leads to a closer consideration of evidence about ways in which family carers construe and make sense of what they do in the support of their child or relative with a disability.

Salutogenic perspectives

In response to the huge literature on stress in families has arisen a body of work that seeks to identify factors contributing to health, resilience and well-being. This is probably traceable to Antonovsky's (1987) seminal work that directs attention to individual, familial and community factors that help people to survive and to make sense of difficult, often non-normative circumstances. Antonovsky's salutogenic thesis suggests that being able to maintain a 'sense of coherence' (SOC) in a challenging world makes the vital difference between staying healthy psychologically or succumbing to life's vicissitudes. He defines SOC as

> 'a global orientation that expresses the extent to which one has a pervasive, enduring though dynamic feeling of confidence that (1) the stimuli deriving from one's internal and external environments in the course of living are structured, predictable, and explicable; (2) the resources are available to one to meet the demands posed by these stimuli; and (3) these demands are challenges, worthy of investment and engagement (p.19)'.

He equates these defining parameters respectively with notions of comprehensibility, manageability and meaningfulness. Repeated life experiences are considered to lead to generalised resistance resources, and increased SOC. For the committed and caring person, he further asserts, 'the way is open to gaining understanding and resources' (p.20).

This perspective has helped to broaden understanding of how individuals and families 'manage' disability well whilst also influencing the working assumptions behind research in related fields such as, for example, child abuse and neglect (Sagy and Dotan 2001) and HIV/Aids (Billings *et al.* 2000). More importantly, it has caused a fundamental re-evaluation of the parameters of transactional stress-coping models (Folkman and Moskowitz 2000), illustrating qualities that are considered to underpin resilience.

Coincidentally, increasing attention has been focussing on sources from which families of children (and adult relatives) with disabilities derive strength and satisfactions from their everyday caring and coping. Discussing these largely as reward factors, Beresford (1994), for example, has reported parents as drawing strength from witnessing their children's successes and achievements or from factors intrinsic to the care giving role. Recognition from professionals also proved to reinforce this general sense of resilience and well-being. Grant *et al.* (1998) have reported similar findings, family care giving uplifts being either intrinsic to the carer (their beliefs and motivations), interpersonal (changed family dynamics) or perceived gains in others, especially the person with disability.

Studies in the US and Canada (amongst others Heller and Factor 1993; Stainton and Besser 1998) add confirmation to these findings and further suggest that it is common for caring to have positive attributions, including an enhanced understanding of life's purpose, a stimulus for personal growth and development, a source of happiness and love, increased tolerance and a positive influence on others in the family and community.

More recently Scorgie and Sobsey (2000) have identified a range of transformational outcomes associated with parenting children with disabilities. Their research suggests that parents perceive personal transformations in relation to acquired roles or acquired traits, relational transformations regarding family relationships, advocacy relationships, friendship networks and attitudes towards people in general, and then finally perspectival transformations which refer to changes in the way people view life. They suggest that such outcomes may not be evident in research in which investigators examine only short-term responses. Citing Palus (1993, p.53) they argue that though challenging events or circumstances tend to produce negative results initially, positive outcomes are 'usually slower to be realised, enduring and of a higher order (eg. a change in values or the ability to form satisfying relationships)'. Folkman's more recent research on partners of men with HIV/Aids has come to similar conclusions (Folkman 1997). These findings suggest that, with respect to motivations and rewards, families can and do take a longer view of their care giving, and that this is integral to how they cope. It is not clear at this point whether professionals fully appreciate this.

Such perspectives can certainly be identified, for example in discerning autobiographies written by families of disabled children (Edelson 2000).

Articulating means and ends in family care giving

From the foregoing accounts it is possible to discern some of the ends to which family carers seem to be striving, implicitly at least, in their everyday care giving. Families may not always be fully conscious of the changing directions of their strivings or of the underlying factors that give rise to these. Perhaps for these reasons policy makers have found it difficult to suggest goals for family support services in other than process terms. For example, in 'Valuing People' (DoH 2001), the new White Paper about people with learning disabilities, it is stated that the challenge is to ensure that carers receive the right support to help them in their caring role, obtain relevant information about services, know who to approach for advice and help, are respected and treated as individuals in their own right and make their voices heard at national and local levels (para 5.3, p.54). It would be perfectly possible for services to be geared to meet these laudable aims but doing so would tell us little about whether this helps families to satisfy the purposes or ends of their care giving efforts. However, research on precisely the latter has helped to shed some welcome light on defining outcomes in social care, including an appreciation of how to address carer-related outcomes with a view to informing service development (Qureshi et al. 2001). Based on focus groups with family carers and a critical appreciation of professional practice, Qureshi and colleagues have proposed a conceptual framework that encourages practitioners to think systematically about four main outcome dimensions from the carer's perspective. Each is considered important to carers and seems to resonate well with the salutogenic thinking described earlier (see also Qureshi, Arksey and Nicholas in this volume).

The first dimension concerns the *quality of life of the person they support* and includes their comfort, appearance, maintenance of maximum independence, attention to safety and security, maintenance of extra-familial social contacts, access to meaningful activity, respect for personal dignity, and improved mobility and morale. In this it reinforces the importance of keeping the disabled child or adult at the heart of the equation since their health and well being, the way they are supported and how they respond all impinge on the sense of accomplishment carers might derive, as others have suggested (Beresford 1994; Grant *et al.* 1998; Scorgie and Sobsey 2000). Maintaining the person's quality of life is very much a primary motivation for caring.

The second dimension concerns *the quality of life of the carer* and is perhaps the most self-evident of the outcome domains, encompassing the carer's physical and emotional well-being, peace of mind, ability to lead a life of their own if they so choose, avoidance of social isolation, maintenance of a positive relationship with the person they are supporting, and adequate material circumstances. Neglect of this dimension by professionals and services is likely to have an impact on a carer's capacity to cope and willingness to continue caring (Shearn and Todd 2000; Walden *et al.* 2000). Families may also need support in balancing care giving and employment (see Ramcharan and Whittell, this volume) as well as their other responsibilities and interests.

The third dimension concerns *recognition and support in the caring role*, expressed in terms of the ability to define the limits of their role, feeling skilled and confident, experiencing satisfaction about a job well done, being able to share responsibility and feel emotional support, and a capacity to manage things. This suggests paying attention to carers' information requirements, preparation for their role, their ways of coping and their capacity to plan ahead (Grant and Whittell 2001; Nolan *et al.* 1996).

The fourth and final dimension of the conceptual framework concerns what Qureshi and colleagues call *process outcomes*. These are to do with the way help is provided and encompass things like being valued and respected as an individual, recognition of one's expertise, involvement in decision making, value for money and a 'good fit' with existing life routines and care giving. A considerable body of literature would support this position (Felce *et al.* 1998; Nolan 2001; Pejlert 2001; Scorgie and Sobsey 2000).

Achieving all this will depend not only on the development of good, informed assessment practice linked to the concerns of families but also on the capacity of front-line professionals to maintain pro-active, helping, empathetic relationships with families and their disabled children or adult offspring.

A large body of research in the US lends weight to the importance of these component parts of family care giving as worthy outcome target areas. The work of Dunst *et al.* (1993, 1994), among others, is probably pre-eminent here, not only because it is so well developed theoretically and empirically but also because the underlying social systems framework causes critical reflection on the dynamics and links between these outcome areas as a direct result of family support interventions. Further, it suggests the need to think about outcomes at different levels: the individual (carer or disabled person), the dyadic (relations between individuals) and the family unit as a whole.

In this connection Williams and Robinson (2001b), for example, have shown that more sensitive forms of assessment are required to appreciate the nature and implications of family dynamics in such cases. Dunst's *et al.* (1993, 1994) work also suggests the need to think about the ways in which structural properties of families (support networks, family forms), relational properties (contact frequency, exchanges and reciprocities) and constitutional properties (types of support, evaluations of support) themselves mediate outcomes at different levels. It suggests a level of sophistication that is worth aiming for but which will severely test measurement and implementation in routine practice.

At last there do seem to be models and emergent assessment technologies capable of testing these links. However, in the UK we are still devoid of systematic evaluations of interventions capable of yielding good evidence of what actually helps families to achieve their goals. There continues to be a high dependency on service process evaluations, consumer surveys of one kind or another, or on qualitative studies of how families care. This will have to change if lessons are to be learned from good practice in supporting or empowering families.

Resilience and expertise in families

A considerable body of literature now illustrates that, with time and experience, families acquire considerable expertise in their varied roles as care manager, planner, direct care provider, advocate, problem solver and gatekeeper (Glendinning 1983; Nolan *et al.* 1996). Investigations of the coping strategies families use to deal with different demands and circumstances show that coping is best when families can draw from a repertoire of coping strategies and match strategies to particular demands. Being able to exploit problem solving and cognitive reframing to the full, instead of using reactive stress reduction tactics, is generally more helpful. A capacity to make sense of what can often be non-normative circumstances appears to be a consistent factor in successful coping. Finally, drawing from different sources of trusted support to help at appropriate times can make the difference between sinking, surviving or swimming (Grant and Whittell 2000; Quine and Pahl 1991; Sloper *et al.* 1991; Todd and Shearn 1996).

Families also make use of strategies to render invisible from their disabled children and relatives many of the things they do on their behalf. These accomplishments appear to be aimed at maintaining the dignity and self-esteem of the 'cared for' person by keeping to a minimum their awareness of things being done on their behalf. Family carers are reported to claim that this invisible work can be very stressful but also rewarding (Grant *et al.* 1998; Nolan *et al.* 1996).

We therefore know much about how families 'do their caring' and also what seems to work for them. The literature is still rather devoid of what disabled children and adults make of these well-intentioned efforts by family members, whether help really helps, what obligations go with being helped and supported, and so on. Factors that may mediate successful coping and management are still being charted. Much more needs to be known about the influence of the structure and dynamics of family support networks, financial and material conditions, culture and ethnicity, and different family forms before more definitive claims about the ingredients of effective coping can be made.

Although therefore we are still discovering what differentiates 'successful' from 'less successful' coping families, a body of knowledge about what might be termed resilience (Hawley and DeHaan 1996) is emerging. If families are to be supported or even empowered, then professionals will need to know a considerable amount about what strengths families have so that these can be acknowledged, learned from and reinforced. It might even be proposed that an assessment of these resilient qualities should be a foundation for intervention in supporting families.

What helps families?

Despite the absence of intervention studies a considerable amount is known about what support families need and want. In crude terms this can be defined in terms of information, respite, psychological support and counselling, in-home training and advocacy (Nolan *et al.* 1996), but what is important in each case is their availability and accessibility, sufficiency, acceptability, timing, flexibility and effectiveness. With the arrival of the still-pervasive contract culture we should also add to this criterion list the costliness of charges of service use to families – although this is typically used as a rationing device it can also be a deterrent.

There continues to be a serious shortfall in sufficient family support services to meet demands, and some groups of families suffer more than others, especially in terms of service accessibility, acceptability and flexibility criteria. This appears to be particularly marked among families from different ethnic backgrounds (Ahmad and Atkin 1996; Hatton *et al.* 1998; Jones *et al.* 2001); families supporting children with challenging behaviours (Hastings and Mount 2001) or medically fragile conditions (Edelson 2000); families where there may be conflicts of interest between family carers and disabled young children or adults (Williams and Robinson 2001a); lone parent or elderly parent families (Grant and Whittell 2000); and family carers trying to hold down jobs (Shearn and Todd 2000; Warfield 2001).

However, there is much to learn about other groups of families not well represented in existing research: reconstituted families, travellers and mobile populations, refugees and recent immigrant families being cases in point. Families where one or both parents have major disabilities as well as children with disabilities represent another cluster about whom relatively little is known. Accommodating such diversity in research but, more especially, in practice remains a major challenge.

Within the body of evidence about what kind of assistance helps families, we know that families value being listened to, being acknowledged as a source of particularistic knowledge and expertise, being able to influence decision making and being able to control the pace at which significant shifts in support or service provision occur (Knox *et al.* 2000; Nolan *et al.* 1996; Stalker 1990). But families also do not want to feel that they have to make all the moves to secure what they need. Rather, evidence suggests that they expect services and professionals to do the running by being more proactive. Arguably the linking factor in all this is the desire of families to maintain control over the vagaries of family support services, sufficient to retain a sense of coherence of a personal and social world that can at times appear disrupted, ambiguous and changing.

Direct payment systems are one means by which disabled people can purchase and control their own support, early evidence for which looks promising (Dawson 2000). How these systems affect reciprocities between disabled people and family members, however, remains to be seen.

Empowerment or support?

Thus far it has been argued that families have been too often victimised, pathologised or marginalised by services. They have in addition occupied ambiguous role-relationships to services. Meanwhile, resources for family support have been lacking, athough the Carers National Strategy (DoH 1999) has provided some hope for the future through new ring-fenced investment dedicated to family support coupled with more 'joined-up' thinking. However, the policy rhetoric has still been couched in terms of *support to* families or else translated into prescriptions about what supports families need, often with little hard evidence about the likelihood of successful outcomes.

Hopefully evidence produced in this chapter thus far has demonstrated at least one important finding, namely that if families are approached in the right way they can identify factors that motivate and reward them in their everyday care giving towards achieving important and realisable goals. Importantly, this suggests that it ought to be possible to sensitise services and professionals to work towards such outcomes on the assumption that these are in the best interests of both families and their disabled children or adult relatives. How might this be accomplished? It is suggested that a model of empowerment applied to families might be one way forward.

In varying degrees a growing body of literature has been pushing thinking beyond merely supporting families who have disabled children to empowering them (Barnes 1997; Case 2000; Clarke 2001; Murray 2000). These commentaries (among many others) make the point that families want to be free from the culture of paternalism that can still pervade services. Further, they argue that families want to be able to negotiate help and support on the basis of working partnerships with professionals, liberated to direct professional attention towards goals and circumstances that they, the family, consider important. At root lies the issue of power relations.

In seeking to conceptualise empowerment Labonté (1993, p.53), cited in Raeburn and Rootman (1996), suggests that it operates simultaneously at three connected levels.

1. At the *intrapersonal level*, it is the experience of a potent sense of self... It is power within, the experience of choice.

2. At the *interpersonal level*, it is power with, the experience of interdependency.

3. At the *intergroup level*, it is the cultivation of resources and strategies for personal and sociopolitical gains, enhancing advocacy and participatory democracy, creating greater social equity: it is power between, the experience of generosity.

Although using health promotion as the backdrop, Labonté (1993) asserts that it is the function of services to enable people to become empowered at each of these levels. He suggests elsewhere (Labonté 1996) that empowerment can exist in two basic forms – as a zero-sum game in which the empowerment of one partner implies some sort of opportunity cost or sacrifice to the other, as for example in the simplistic notion of professionals transferring power to service users or families – or as a non zero-sum game which implies the wider transformational powers of partnership practice where individuals, families and wider communities of interest all participate and derive benefits. This is much in line with other commentators (Clarke 2001; Fisher 1994, for example) who suggest that services should be thinking beyond a preoccupation with empowerment merely as a vehicle to engage people in decision making and move towards an ecological model that seeks to link psychological (individual) empowerment with influence at organisational and community levels. There are others, however, that remain sceptical about the capacity of services to empower at all (Dowson 1997).

A final point to be made here about the idea of empowerment is that it can be articulated both as a set of processes or as an outcome of activities and practices. Although this suggests that, as a multilevel construct, empowerment is complex, it does nevertheless suggest that closer attention be paid to the links between processes and outcomes. Does, for example, an attempt to increase a carer's control over assessment and care management processes lead to better outcomes for carers (self-esteem, self-efficacy), the family as a whole (family cohesion) or the disabled child (personal development, family integration)? In this there are dangers that over-zealous moves to involve and consult families will overwhelm many, with risks that they may withdraw from individual care planning (or its equivalent) as well as from other planning arenas (Felce *et al.* 1998).

With such caveats in mind, Table 5.1 is an attempt to characterise and compare basic elements of traditional family support with an approach to family empowerment. The left-hand side of the table lists a range of parameters to be considered in both models and the reader is invited to read across from these.

Table 5.1 Contrastive models of family support

Parameter	Model of family support	
	Traditional support	Empowerment led
Professional knowledge base	Individualised casework	Family systems models
View of family as resource	Autonomy of individual members	Reciprocities and individual autonomy Support for roles beyond caregiving
Authority base	Professional as expert Professional as case manager	Family as expert Family as case manager
Predominating view of 'the family'	Pathogenic	Salutogenic
Assessment	Needs driven Process oriented	Strengths, wishes and dreams-led outcome – and process oriented
Source of solution	Services	Family/community resources supported by services facilitating linkage between intrapersonal, interpersonal and intergroup levels
Perspective	Crisis management Short-term imperatives	Importance of temporal factors in family care and long-term planning
Decision making approach	Zero-sum game	Non zero-sum game
Pacing	Dictated by services	Dictated by family
Organisational	Formal/bureaucratic	Organic, network-driven

Taking each in turn, it is suggested that a family systems framework represents a useful initial sensitising for empowerment practice in that it will help to highlight the structure of supportive ties within families and reciprocities between family members, including the disabled child. At the same time, it recognises that family members are likely to have roles and responsibilities that impact upon their care giving but which lie outside of what goes on in the household (employment, schooling of other children, care of other relatives for example).

It is suggested that families are regarded as repositories of expertise (or potentially so) and that they will develop lots of experience in (informal) case management roles from which services, if they are to work in partnership, can only learn. This in turn requires that a salutogenic view be taken of families in general, which is not to suggest that families will not encounter difficult challenges from time to time. Rather, it is to suggest that an optimistic and long-term view be taken about what families can (and do) accomplish for themselves and their children with disabilities.

In relation to assessment a family-led approach is advocated since this is more likely to bring out important self-determined strengths, wishes and even dreams. This will require a reordering of thinking by professionals and support workers about the appropriateness of needs-led assessment formulae. In seeking to solve problems, the model would suggest that family and community resources should be the primary focus in order to promote a sense of control and a close identity with local supportive constituencies of interest (other families, self-help groups, community agencies, for example), and that the aim would be to enable family members to develop competencies and the self-confidence to exploit these local resources. In so doing they may begin to achieve a sense of empowerment suggested by Labonté's (1993) model.

A long-term view is required so that families can be helped to realise the kinds of transitions that will occur over the lifespan and to plan for these. Being involved in making this happen (decision making) involves, it is suggested, a non zero-sum game in which supports, expertise and knowledge, as well as external resources, can multiply in such a way that disabled children, their families and the community will all derive benefits. Empowerment, if it is to work, cannot be rushed. Families will have to be prepared to take ownership of the processes and dictate the pace of change.

What we need now is some good UK examples of empowering family support practices so that robust evaluations can be undertaken.

References

Ahmad, W.I.U. and Atkin, K. (1996) 'Ethnicity and caring for a disabled child: The case of children with sickle cell or thalassaemia.' *British Journal of Social Work 26*, 755–775.

Antonovsky, A. (1987) *Unravelling the Mystery of Health.* San Francisco CA: Jossey Bass.

Ashworth, M. and Baker, A.H. (2000) '"Time and space": Carers' views about respite care.' *Health and Social Care in the Community 8*, 1, 50–56.

Barnes, M. (1997) 'Families and empowerment.' In P. Ramcharan, G. Roberts, G. Grant and J. Borland (eds) *Empowerment in Everyday Life: Learning Disability.* London: Jessica Kingsley Publishers.

Beresford, B. (1994) *Positively Parents: Caring for a Severely Disabled Child.* London: HMSO.

Bigby, C. (1997) 'When parents relinquish care: Informal support networks of older people with intellectual disability.' *Journal of Applied Research in Intellectual Disabilities 10*, 4, 333–344.

Billings, D.W., Folkman, S., Acree, M. and Moskowitz, J.T. (2000) 'Coping and physical health during caregiving: The roles of positive and negative affect.' *Journal of Personality and Social Psychology 79*, 1, 131–142.

Case, S. (2000) 'Refocusing on the parent: What are the social issues of concern for parents of disabled children?' *Disability and Society 15*, 2, 271–292.

Clarke, N. (2001) 'Training as a vehicle to empower carers in the community: More than a question of information sharing.' *Health and Social Care in the Community 9*, 2, 79–88.

Cotterill, L., Hayes, L., Flynn, M. and Sloper, P. (1997) 'Reviewing respite services: Some lessons from the literature.' *Disability and Society 12*, 5, 775–788.

Dawson, C. (2000) *Independent Successes: Implementing Direct Payments.* York: York Publishing Services.

DoH (Department of Health) (1999) *Caring about Carers: A National Strategy for Carers.* London: HMSO.

DoH (Department of Health) (2001) *Valuing People: A New Strategy for Learning Disability for the 21st Century.* Cm 5086. London: HMSO.

Dowson, S. (1997) 'Empowerment within services: A comfortable delusion.' In P. Ramcharan, G. Roberts, G. Grant and J. Borland (eds) *Empowerment in Everyday Life: Learning Disability.* London: Jessica Kingsley Publishers, pp. 101-120.

Dunst, C.J., Trivette, C.M. and Deal, A.G. (1994) *Supporting and Strengthening Families: Vol.1, Methods, Strategies and Practices.* Cambridge MA: Brookline Books.

Dunst, C.J., Trivette, C.M., Starnes, A.L., Hamby, D.W. and Gordon, N.J. (1993) *Building and Evaluating Family Support Initiatives.* Baltimore MD: Paul H. Brookes.

Edelson, M. (2000) *My Journey with Jake: A Memoir of Parenting and Disability.* Toronto: Between the Lines.

Felce, D., Grant, G., Todd, S., Ramcharan, P., Beyer, S., McGrath, M., Perry, J., Shearn, J., Kilsby, M. and Lowe, K. (1998) *Towards a Full Life: Researching Policy Innovation for People with Learning Disabilities.* Oxford: Butterworth Heinemann.

Fisher, M. (1994) 'Partnership practice and empowerment.' In P. Nurius and L. Gutierriez (eds) *Education and Research for Empowerment Practice.* Washington: University of Washington.

Folkman, S. (1997) 'Positive psychological states and coping with severe stress.' *Social Science and Medicine 45,* 1207–1221.

Folkman, S. and Moskowitz, J.T. (2000) 'Positive affect and the other side of coping.' *American Psychologist 55,* 6, 647–654.

Glendinning, C. (1983) *Unshared Care: Parents and their Disabled Children.* London: Routledge and Kegan Paul.

Grant, G. (1990) 'Elderly parents with handicapped children: Anticipating the future.' *Journal of Aging Studies 4,* 4, 359–374.

Grant, G. and Ramcharan, P. (2001) 'Views and experiences of people with intellectual disabilities and their families: (2) The family perspective.' *Journal of Applied Research in Intellectual Disabilities 14,* 364–380.

Grant, G., Ramcharan, P., McGrath, M., Nolan, M. and Keady, J. (1998) 'Rewards and gratifications among family caregivers: Towards a refined model of caring and coping.' *Journal of Intellectual Disability Research 42,* 1, 58–71.

Grant, G. and Whittell, B. (2000) 'Differentiated coping strategies in families with children and adults with intellectual disabilities: The relevance of gender, family composition and the lifespan.' *Journal of Applied Research in Intellectual Disabilities 13,* 4, 256–275.

Grant, G. and Whittell, B. (2001) 'Do families and care managers have a similar view of family coping?' *Journal of Learning Disabilities 5,* 2, 111–120.

Hastings, R.P. and Mount, R.H. (2001) 'Early correlates of behavioural and emotional problems in children and adolescents with severe intellectual disabilities: A preliminary study.' *Journal of Applied Research in Intellectual Disabilities 14,* 4, 381–391.

Hatton, C., Azmi, S., Caine, A. and Emerson, E. (1998) 'Informal carers of adolescents and adults with learning difficulties from the south Asian communities: Family circumstances, service support and carer stress.' *British Journal of Social Work 28,* 821–837.

Hawley, D. and DeHaan, L. (1996) 'Towards a definition of family resilience: Integrating life-span and family perspectives.' *Family Process 35,* 283–298.

Helff, C.M. and Glidden, L.M. (1998) 'More positive or less negative? Trends in research on adjustment of families having children with developmental disabilities.' *Mental Retardation 36*, 6, 457–464.

Heller, T. and Factor, A. (1993) 'Support systems, well-being and placement decision-making among older parents and their adult children with developmental disabilities.' In E. Sutton, A. Factor, B.A. Hawkins, A. Heller and G.B. Seltzer (eds) *Older Adults with Developmental Disabilities: Optimising Choice and Change.* Baltimore MD: Paul H. Brookes.

Heller, T., Miller, A.B. and Factor, A. (1997) 'Adults with mental retardation as supports to their parents: Effects on parental caregiving appraisal.' *Mental Retardation 35*, 5, 338–346.

Henwood, M. (1998) *Ignored and Invisible? Carers' Experience of the NHS.* Report of a UK research survey commissioned by the Carers' National Association.

Jones, L., Atkin, K. and Ahmad, W.I.U. (2001) 'Supporting Asian deaf young people and their families: The role of professionals and services.' *Disability and Society 16*, 1, 51–70.

Knox, M., Parmenter, T., Atkinson, N. and Yazbeck, M. (2000) 'Family control: The views of families who have a child with an intellectual disability.' *Journal of Applied Research in Intellectual Disabilities 13*, 17–28.

Labonté, R. (1996) 'Measurement and practice: Power issues in quality of life, health promotion and empowerment.' In R. Renwick, I. Brown and M. Nagler (eds) *Quality of Life in Health Promotion and Rehabilitation: Conceptual Approaches, Issues, and Applications.* Thousand Oaks: Sage.

McGrath, M. and Grant, G. (1993) 'The life cycle and support networks of families with a mentally handicapped member' *Disability, Handicap and Society 8*, 25–41.

Male, D.B. (1998) 'Parents' views about special provision for their child with severe or profound and multiple learning difficulties.' *Journal of Applied Research in Intellectual Disabilities 11*, 2, 129–145.

Murray, P. (2000) 'Disabled children, parents and professionals: Partnership on whose terms?' *Disability and Society 15*, 4, 683–698.

Nolan, M. (2001) 'Working with family carers: Towards a partnership approach.' *Reviews in Clinical Gerontology 11*, 91–97.

Nolan, M. and Grant, G. (1992) *Regular Respite: An Examination of a Hospital Rota Bed Scheme for Elderly People.* London: Ace Books.

Nolan, M., Grant, G. and Keady, J. (1996) *Understanding Family Care: A Multidimensional Model of Caring and Coping.* Buckingham: Open University Press.

Palus, C.J. (1993) 'Transformative experiences of adulthood: A new look at the seasons of life.' In J. Demeck, K. Bursik and R. Dibiase (eds) Parental Development. Hillsdale NJ: Erlbaum, pp.39–58.

Pejlert, A. (2001) 'Being a parent of an adult son or daughter with severe mental illness receiving professional care: Parents' narratives.' *Health and Social Care in the Community 9*, 4, 194–204.

Prosser, H. (1997) 'The future care plans of older adults with intellectual disabilities living at home with family carers.' *Journal of Applied Research in Intellectual Disabilities 10*, 1, 15–32.

Quine, L. and Pahl, J. (1991) 'Stress and coping in mothers caring for a child with severe learning difficulties: A test of Lazarus' transactional model of coping.' *Journal of Community and Applied Social Psychology 1*, 57–70.

Qureshi, H., Bamford, C., Nicholas, E., Patmore, C. and Harris, J. (2001) *Outcomes in Social Care Practice: Developing an Outcome Focus in Care Management and User Surveys.* York: University of York, Social Policy Research Unit. See Chapter 4, Implementing an Outcomes Approach in Carer Assessment and Review.

Raeburn, J.M. and Rootman, I. (1996) *Quality of Life and Health Promotion.* In R. Renwick, I. Brown and M. Nagler (eds) *Quality of Life in Health Promotion and Rehabilitation: Conceptual Approaches, Issues, and Applications.* Thousand Oaks: Sage.

Ramcharan, P., Robert, G., Grant, G. and Borland, J. (eds) (1997) *Empowerment in Everyday Life: Learning Disability.* London: Jessica Kingsley Publishers. Reprinted 2000.

Robinson, C. and Williams, V. (1999) *In Their Own Right.* Bristol: Norah Fry Research Centre, University of Bristol.

Sagy, S. and Dotan, N. (2001) 'Coping resources of maltreated children in the family: A salutogenic approach.' *Child Abuse and Neglect 25*, 1463–1480.

Scorgie, K. and Sobsey, D. (2000) 'Transformational outcomes associated with parenting children who have disabilities.' *Mental Retardation 38*, 3, 195–206.

Shearn, J. and Todd, S. (2000) 'Maternal employment and family responsibilities: The perspectives of mothers of children with intellectual disabilities.' *Journal of Applied Research in Intellectual Disabilities 13*, 109–131.

Simpson, M. (2001) 'Programming adulthood: Intellectual disability and adult services.' In D. May (ed) *Transition and Change in the Lives of People with Intellectual Disabilities.* London: Jessica Kingsley Publishers, pp. 97–116.

Sloper, T., Knussen, C., Turner, S. and Cunningham, C.C. (1991) 'Factors related to stress and satisfaction in life with families of children with Down Syndrome.' *Journal of Child Psychology and Psychiatry 32*, 655–676.

Stainton, T. and Besser, H. (1998) 'The positive impact of children with an intellectual disability on the family.' *Journal of Intellectual and Developmental Disability 23*, 57–70.

Stalker, K. (1990) *Share the Care: An Evaluation of a Family-Based Respite Care Service.* London: Jessica Kingsley Publishers.

Todd, S. and Shearn, J. (1996) 'Time and the person: The impact of support services on the lives of parents of adults with learning disabilities.' *Journal of Applied Research in Intellectual Disabilities 9*, 40–60.

Twigg, J. (2000) 'The changing role of users and carers.' In B. Hudson (ed) *The Changing Role of Social Care.* London: Jessica Kingsley Publishers, pp. 103–119.

Twigg, J. and Atkin, K. (1994) *Carers Perceived: Policy and Practice in Informal Care.* Buckingham: Open University Press.

Walden, S., Pistrang, N. and Joyce, T. (2000) 'Parents of adults with intellectual disabilities: Quality of life and experience of caring.' *Journal of Applied Research in Intellectual Disabilities 13*, 62–76.

Warfield, M.E. (2001) 'Employment, parenting and well-being among mothers of children with disabilities.' *Mental Retardation 39*, 4, 297–309.

Warfield, M.E. and Hauser-Cram, P. (1996) 'Child care needs, arrangements and satisfactions of mothers with children with developmental disabilities.' *Mental Retardation 34*, 5, 294–302.

Warner, C. and Wexler, S. (1998) *Eight Hours a Day and Taken For Granted?* London: Princess Royal Trust for Carers.

Williams, V. and Robinson, C. (2001a) 'More than one wavelength: Identifying, understanding and resolving conflicts of interest between people with intellectual disabilities and their family carers.' *Journal of Applied Research in Intellectual Disabilities 14*, 30–46.

Williams, V. and Robinson, C. (2001b) '"He will finish up caring for me": People with learning disabilities and mutual care.' *British Journal of Learning Disabilities 29*, 56–62.

CHAPTER 6

Caring Voices
Carers' Participation in Policy and Practice
Helen Rogers and Marian Barnes

Introduction

The involvement of carers in decision making about service delivery, and in broader issues of service planning and evaluation, is one dimension of a widespread commitment to user and citizen involvement in public policy (for example, Lowndes, Pratchett and Stoker 1998). Contemporary policy discourse embraces the concepts of partnership, empowerment, consultation and inclusivity. Irrespective of the substantive aspect of caring, the practice of service planners and providers, in principle at least, is open to scrutiny and influence by carers. This emphasis, which gained momentum with the implementation of the NHS and Community Care Act 1990, the Carers (Recognition and Services) Act 1995 and the National Carers Strategy (1999), reflects a broader trend towards participatory rights and responsibilities of citizenship and participatory democracy (Barnes and Prior 2000; Prior, Stewart and Walsh 1995). Further, it is an emphasis that aspires to put government in touch with people and promotes the social inclusion of those traditionally marginalised within the power structures of society (DETR 1998, 1999).

The rhetoric, however, does little to illuminate the complex and multidimensional factors that surround the engagement of carers with service planners and providers. Equally, it is silent on the challenges that participation and consultation might uncover in terms of organisational and professional politics. In addition, whilst carers are recognised as somehow distinct from 'users' of services, the tendency to elide 'users and carers' within partic- ipation initiatives conceals the complexity of the triangular relationship between paid service providers, those who are on the receiving end of health and social care services, and family members, friends or lovers who provide help and support to them.

This chapter explores national policy objectives in relation to carer in- volvement. Yet, as we will argue, recognising carers' voices does not assume that what is being said is either listened or responded to. In reviewing research in this area one purpose, therefore, is to explore the reasons for this apparent mismatch. We begin by briefly summarising how the role of carers as a social group, and one which has subsequently been the focus of public policy, has been recognised through collective action. In particular, we note how the outcomes of this collective action have helped to shape the current policy environment. From here we take a temporary, but necessary, departure away from the notion of collective action to consider whether the experience of care giving is necessarily associated with accepting an identity as a 'carer'. Following on from this, we discuss how different models are used to explain the ambiguous position of carers *vis-à-vis* service planners and providers. We then look at different types of participation and the outcomes this has (or is intended to have) on service developments.

The development of carers' organisations

Carers have been involved in collective action since well before official com- munity care policy started to give recognition to the part played by family and friends in supporting older people, disabled people and others who were the focus of such policy. In the early 1960s the Reverend Mary Webster, an unmarried woman who had given up her work in the early 1950s to care for her elderly parents, established the National Council for the Single Woman and her Dependants (NCSWD) (McKenzie 1995). Throughout the 1960s and 1970s NCSWD lobbied, researched and held conferences in order to draw attention to the needs of single women caring for elderly parents. The successes of the NCSWD, which included the intro- duction of the Attendance Allowance in 1971 and the Invalid Care Allowance in 1976, prompted married, divorced and widowed women to seek support from the organisation which subsequently became known as the National Council for Carers and their Elderly Dependants (NCCED). (See Barnes 1997a, 2002 for more detailed discussions of the emergence of collective action amongst carers.)

In 1981, the Association of Carers was founded to represent all carers irrespective of age, gender, marital status or their relationship to the person they cared for. Some members of the NCCED were unhappy at this broadening of the remit and the NCCED remained as a separate organisation until 1988 when the two organisations merged to form the National Carers Association. Now known as Carers UK, the National Carers Association is well established as the national voice of carers and there are regional and local groups throughout the UK which campaign for and provide support to carers in diverse circumstances.

Official recognition of carers

There is a substantial body of research which has explored the experience of caring and the relationship between 'informal' care and 'professional' care provision (see Parker 1990; Twigg, Atkin and Perring 1990, for reviews of this research). This research contributed to the official recognition of the importance of lay care if community care policy was to be effective. The extent to which community care policy was dependent on the preparedness of family members and others to provide support for disabled, ill and frail relatives and friends was clearly indicated in the Griffiths Report and the subsequent White Paper which preceded the 1990 NHS and Community Care Act.

> Publicly funded services constitute only a small part of the total care provided to people in need. Families, friends, neighbours and other local people provide the majority of care in response to needs which they are uniquely placed to identify and respond to. This will continue to be the primary means by which people are enabled to live normal lives in community settings. The proposal takes as its starting point that this is as it should be. And that the first task of publicly provided services is to support

and where possible strengthen these networks of carers. (Griffiths 1988, p.5)

While this White Paper focuses largely on the role of statutory and independent bodies in the provision of community care services, the reality is that most care is provided by family, friends and neighbours... Helping carers to maintain their valuable contribution to the spectrum of care is both right and a sound investment. (Secretaries of State 1989, 2–3)

While it was clearly in the interests of the state to recognise the role played by carers, there is also some ambiguity in the relationship between service providers and carers. Twigg and Atkin (1994) suggest:

They [carers] lie on the margins of the social care system; in one sense within its remit, part of its concerns and responses; in another, beyond its remit, part of the taken-for-granted reality against which welfare services operate. (Twigg and Atkin 1994, p.11)

Twigg and Atkin (1994) have identified four ways in which service providers respond to carers: carers as resources, carers as co-workers, carers as co-clients and superseded carers.

Carers as resources

In the 'carers as resource model' the term carer embraces a broad spectrum with no distinctions made between help given by friends, neighbours or those closely involved in a care-giving relationship. The cared-for person is at the centre of this model with carers featuring as part of the background and as a resource to be drawn on to provide support. The needs of the carer may be of interest to agencies, but only take on more significance when the carer is having difficulty coping and needs support from formal care providers. In this model, we can expect little commitment to consultation with carers about their own needs.

Carers as co-workers

In the second of Twigg and Atkin's (1994) models informal carers are seen as working alongside formal carers. Here the interweaving of skills and attributes is seen as transcending the informal/formal divide. In practice, however, attempts to co-work have been problematic, primarily because of the discordant assumptions that underlie the two systems (Abrams 1985; Bulmer 1987). In this model the main focus of attention is still the person who is being cared for, but the carer is assigned a more important role than the previous model suggests. This encompasses the carer's interests and well-being within its parameters but on an ostensibly instrumental basis. Conflicts of interest are recognised, but are usually subsumed under an assumption that carers want to care and that the most effective way of developing relationships with carers is to assist them in this regard. In this context carer involvement may be seen as a process of negotiating 'who does what'.

Carers as co-clients

Use of the term here is narrow and focuses on carers who are heavily involved in caring. This model embraces the possibility that carers also have needs which should be met alongside those of the primary clients. This includes a recognition that the needs of carers may conflict with those of the direct service user and there may be some tension between the priority given to carer and user involvement.

Superseded carers

Twigg and Atkin (1994) suggest that workers who adopt this model aim not to support or underwrite the care-giving relationship but to transcend or supersede it. They suggest that there are two routes through which this might be achieved. The first starts from a concern with the cared-for person and with maximising their independence. The other is to intervene in ways which reduce and possibly eliminate reliance on the carer. The aim in the first route is not to relieve the carer, but to free the person from the dependant relationship. They suggest that this model is influential in work with people with learning disabilities, physical disabilities and mental health problems. The second route is that by maximising the independence of the person, the carers' 'services' can be disposed of. Carers in this model tend to be described as relatives or 'friends', utilising more neutral terms which do not imply some level of obligations and responsibilities. Carer and person are seen as independent, with potential conflict being recognised, and user involvement is likely to be prioritised over carer involvement.

Recognition of the different and sometimes conflicting interests of service users and carers has been an important theme within initiatives which seek to enable those on the receiving end of services to have their say about them. For example, during the 1980s the All Wales Strategy for People with Mental Handicap (as it was then called) sought to involve people with learning difficulties and their families in planning the development of a different model of service. In practice it was usually family members rather than people with learning difficulties who were involved directly. McGrath (1989) and Grant (1992), who researched these developments, argued that it was important to recognise this when considering the proposals emanating from these involvement initiatives.

However, others have also emphasised the reciprocity often involved in relationships between carers and those to whom they provide support and, in some cases, the difficulty of determining who is the carer and who the person cared for (Qureshi and Walker 1989). This applies in particular in the case of older people who may provide support to each other through illness or frailty (Rummery 2001). But it can also apply in the case of, for example, people with learning difficulties who act to support elderly parents or who become parents themselves (Booth and Booth 1994).

Do carers see themselves as carers?

The establishment of organisations representing the interests of carers required the naming of carers as a group, and of caring as an activity deserving of recognition by policy makers. Thus, one of the aims of such organisations has been to encourage people providing support to relatives or friends to identify themselves as 'carers'. But not all are happy to accept this identity. Various factors influence the way carers see themselves. First, the contemporary use of the term 'carer' has been developed within social care agencies and it bears the mark of that origin (Twigg, Atkin and Perrin 1990). Carers frequently assert that they do not see themselves as such; the term is unfamiliar to them and, some would argue, at odds with how they perceive their actions. They regard these as an extension of family or personal relations rather than in terms of being a carer with its formal, quasi-employment overtones. Second, and following on from this point, there is no simple definition of being a carer. Conceptually, the term centres on the performance of tasks, which are both supportive in nature and are grounded in pre-existing relationships of kinship or friendship (Thomas 1993). It is, however, often difficult to distinguish such carer relations from the ordinary patterns of care and interdependency characteristic of interpersonal, family and gender relations. At what point, therefore, does a partner, son, daughter or neighbour cease being such in order to formally take on or be assigned the role of carer? Third, carers are 'not a homogenous group, nor are they a static group' (Becker 2000, p.27). Research suggests that a claim to the contrary ignores important differences in the experiences of women and men carers (Ungerson 1987), of Black carers (Atkin 1991; Chamba, *et al.* 1999), and those caring for partners rather than for parents or children (Parker 1990). In addition there is the extent to which caring is experienced as a 'burden' (Braithewaite 1990) or as a source of identity and purpose (Nolan, Grant and Keady 1996). Carers may share a common ground deriving from the activity of care giving, but the impact on their lives in respect of financial and employment sacrifices (Seddon 1999), the loss of a social life, friends and freedom and adapting to a new role, will be different in each case (see, for example, Archbold 1983; Barnes *et al.* 1981; Dunkle 1985). Finally, as we have argued above, there is some fluidity between the role of carer and service user. Whilst we recognise the different challenges faced by carers, in considering evidence about carer involvement in and contribution to service development and delivery we take a generic approach – not least because little work has been done in this area which directly explores differences between carers in the nature of their involvement in decision making.

Research and experience indicate that it is important to distinguish the voice of carers from that of service users, and to be clear about the expectations of any initiative which seeks to involve carers in discussion about services or policy. We need to be able to distinguish between carers speaking on their own behalf about their own needs, and circumstances in which they are speaking on behalf of those for whom they provide care and support. In the latter case it is important to understand whether they have been author-ised to act as advocates for others.

The policy context and the impact of carer involvement

The 1980s and 1990s saw an increasingly high profile for the role played by carers and the development of a number of initiatives through which carers were making an impact on policy and practice. In 1985, following an initiative launched by the Department of Health under the heading 'Helping the Community to Care', the King's Fund Informal Caring Unit was estab-lished. This unit combined information giving and gathering, research and service development. Ten years later the Carers' Impact, the successor to the Caring Unit and an alliance of local authority, health authority and volun-tary sector organisations, held its first national conference entitled 'Carers in the Mainstream?' These initiatives focused on community care and the role of carers within them. The focus on the financial circumstances which had been the primary concern of the NCSWD continued to be pursued by the Association of Carers (AoC) in the 'Caring Costs' campaign and, in particular, the need to extend the Invalid Care Allowance to married and co-habitating women. This was achieved following an appeal to the European Court of Justice in 1986.

While the 'Caring Costs' campaign continued to emphasise the personal and financial implications of caring and the amount which informal carers save the State by providing unpaid care, during the latter part of the 1980s attention shifted to the policy review process which culminated in the passage of the NHS and Community Care Act 1990. Much of the work of the AoC, and subsequently of the Carers National Association, can be seen as making authorities aware that it is not only the direct service user who has needs which should be met, but also that carers have needs which should be both taken into account and responded to.

Barnes (1997a) has argued that the success of the carers' lobby in gaining access to senior policy makers during the debates leading up to the 1990 Act hinges on the fact that it was in the Government's interest to ensure carers continued to be prepared to provide support to disabled and older rel-atives. Jill Pitkeathly, the founder member of the Carers Impact Steering

Group, was invited to become a member of the group advising Roy Griffiths as he worked on the report commissioned by the Department of Health, *Community Care: Agenda for Action*. This report showed strong evidence of normative assumptions about the value of care by family and friends, and placed public services in a supportive role to this.

While campaigning activity continued to operate at national level, local examples of influential action by carers started to emerge. For example, the Birmingham Community Care Special Action Project (CCSPA) gave particular prominence to carer involvement as part of a three-year initiative to achieve 'user-led community care' in the city (see Barnes 1997a and Barnes and Wistow 1993 for details of this). The start of the Birmingham project predated the 1990 Act and government ministers were amongst those who visited CCSAP to hear carers' views about how services should develop. A long-term result of this initiative was the establishment of carers' panels and a carers' unit to continue to provide a forum within which carers' voices could be heard.

Subsequent to the 1990 Act carers have not only been lobbying from outside the system, but are increasingly being invited to take part in decision making by service providers. One of the outcomes of this was the enactment of the Carers (Recognition and Services) Act 1995. The Act is a landmark in social policy legislation since it gives people who are providing, or who are intending to provide, regular and substantial care the right to an assessment of their ability to care when the person requiring support is being assessed for community care services.

Recognising the significance of carers' roles in terms of service development and provision culminated in the publication of the National Carers Strategy (1999). This document reinforces the rhetoric that New Labour is committed to providing continuing support to carers on the basis that the Government 'values what they do' (HM Goverment 1999, p.5).

In what is described as a substantial policy package about carers, the Government recognises some of the key factors that have been reported in research findings for the last decade or so. These are summarised as three elements of the strategy and include:

1.   *Information* – a new charter on what people can expect from
      long-term care services; setting new standards; deliberations on
      how to improve the consistency of charging for services;
      accessible health information; NHS direct helpline for carer
      information and government information on the internet.

2.   *Support* – the involvement of carers in planning and providing
      services; consultation with local 'caring' organisations; comment
      cards; advice surgeries; and carers' weeks.

3.   *Care* – carers' right to have their own health needs met; new
      powers for local authorities to provide services for carers, as well
      as for those being cared for; and a new grant to help carers to
      take a break.

This suggests that there has been a preparedness on the part of policy
makers to respond to the carers' lobby. In the next section we consider, in
more detail, both what has been learnt about the practice of carer participation and what these carers who have been involved have been saying about
community care services.

The practice of participation

The practice of carer involvement can be understood as operating on three
levels. First, as working with carers to establish their own needs and, consequently, their access to services. It is at the point of assessment that there can
be tensions between user involvement and carer involvement in determining
an appropriate balance of support and in negotiating roles within a caring
relationship (Ellis 1993). The process of assessment, and subsequently care
planning and review, should involve discussions and agreement on what has
been decided at any one point. While there are constraining influences in
what Braye (2000, p.18) calls the 'consumerist model', in terms of eligibility
criteria and budget limitations, this approach is underpinned by the
principles of accessibility and availability of information, choice, redress and
representation. Yet a study focusing on the local implementation of the
Carers (Recognition and Services) Act 1995 found that these principles
were not also recognisable in practice (Arksey, Hepworth and Qureshi

2000). In a sample of 51 carers, all of whom had recently had an assessment of their needs, about half did not fully realise that they had been assessed at all. Forty-seven of the carers interviewed, who provided care for more than 35 hours per week, had limited knowledge of the Carers Act and their entitlements despite policy guidance to staff explicitly stating that carers should be told about their rights. This suggests there has been little change from earlier assessment experiences of users and carers reported by Davis *et al.* (1997).

A second area where participation and consultation with carers takes place is in the strategic planning of service provision and development. Rather than focusing on individual use of services, the strategic planning arena is more concerned with broader and thus more general features of provision. The role of carers may be to offer a perspective on specific aspects of services informed by their own experience and expertise, or to act as representatives of a carer's group or organisation which has an interest in a particular area (see for example McGrath 1989; Barnes and Wistow 1993, 1994). Alternatively, carers may comprise part of a wider planning and con-sultative network rather than a single planning forum. In either case, consul-tation may take place through a range of mechanisms – workshops, meetings, surveys, focus groups and so on – in order to elicit their views and take them into account for future service development.

A third area where participation with carers is encouraged is through research projects. From this perspective, carers are not seen as 'subjects' but rather as 'co-researchers' taking on some responsibility for setting the research agenda and actively contributing to the evaluation of services. (For examples relating to young carers see Frank, Tatum and Tucker 1999 and Newton and Becker 1999 . For an example relating to carers of older people with dementia see Rogers 2000). At a basic level the experiences of carers have increasingly been seen as valid contributions to the development of service providers' knowledge and understanding about the need for, and the use of, health and social care services.

The 'one-off' consultation events which characterised much of the early carer involvement initiatives, including the first stage of the Birmingham Community Care Special Action Project (Barnes and Wistow 1992), have increasingly been recognised as inadequate if there is to be a real dialogue which can lead to sustainable change. Thus the establishment of standing panels which enable carers to meet regularly with each other, as well as to both initiate dialogue and respond to consultative approaches from officials, have been an important means of overcoming charges of tokenism in consultation. Barnes and Wistow (1993) identified a number of ways in which carers taking part in ongoing carers panels received direct benefits from this involvement:

- The meetings were an opportunity to provide and receive personal support from each other.

- They were an opportunity for information sharing between carers.

- As carers got to know each other the panels provided a safe environment in which they could explore difficult experiences.

- For some, the meetings were an important social event.

- They were a means of accessing information to help them resolve immediate problems.

- Carers developed skills and self-confidence to speak up on their own and others' behalf.

There are, however, a number of factors that deter carers from taking part in strategic deliberations. Drawing on the findings of a range of studies (Barnes and Wistow 1993, 1994; Hoyes et al. 1993; Humpreys 1987), these factors can be summarised as follows:

- The pressures of caring can make it difficult to take part, particularly if there is no sitting service.

- Some older carers may have well-established routines of care and therefore have little desire for change in existing support or service provision.

- Some carers, who have played an active role in carers' issues earlier in their lives, may wish to make way for younger carers.

- A lack of clarity or appropriateness of information accompanying planning meetings can deter carers from taking part.

- Some carers distance themselves from service providers if they perceive them to have uncaring or disinterested attitudes.

- Maintaining motivation to participate becomes difficult if tangible benefits from participation are not forthcoming.

- Carers need to feel supported in the process of participation. This support is even more important if carers have not been used to being asked for their opinions and views.

Despite these deterrents, carers do engage with service planners and providers even though they may see no immediate or direct effect in terms of service change. Whilst there was often frustration amongst carers involved in the Birmingham panels at the slow pace of change, it was important to them that they were at last being recognised as having expertise that was valuable to paid service providers. And as one of the panel members said: 'You can't be influential unless you're in the system and you know what goes on behind closed doors' (Barnes and Wistow 1993, p.47). Braye (2000, p.18) suggests this 'democratic model of participation is about participation with the purpose of achieving greater influence and control'. It can be important to feel that your voice is being heard and valued, and to feel that it is possible to influence change as well as to see change in practice.

Humpreys's (1987) study of carers' involvement in the All Wales Strategy identified different motivations amongst carers who became involved in this initiative. He described both 'democratic radicals' and 'patient participators' amongst those who took part. The democratic radicals were a number of participants who were:

> sustained in their efforts by an element of political idealism: a desire to make hitherto apparently autonomous officers within service providing agencies more accountable to the mandators – this is the wishes of parents of the mentally handicapped [*sic*]. The AWS which stresses the need for parents and other interested parties to be consulted and listened to, provided them with a legitimate platform and thereby encouraged a latent political force which may be termed democratic radicalism. (Humpreys 1987, p.31)

These individuals demanded an equal platform with service providers and, on occasions, when they were frustrated with their aim, adopted political tactics including the use of the media to seek support for their position.

The 'patient participators', on the other hand, were not considered to bring a political perspective to their involvement in the strategy, but were people who brought their experiential knowledge and the wishes of their sons and daughters to bear on multi-agency service planning and development. As they became more aware of the bureaucratic structures and processes, they were able to make an increasing contribution. However, unlike the radicals, they were more content to remain as junior partners and thus were considered less threatening to the status quo.

There are always likely to be a range of different objectives to be pursued through carer involvement initiatives. As we have seen, carers have their own reasons for getting involved and may achieve a range of benefits from their involvement which may not directly equate with the purposes for which such initiatives were established. Ongoing initiatives are dynamic and there may be a shift in the remit and purpose of groups over time. For example, as the Birmingham Carers' Panels pursued their original remit of monitoring action that had been promised in response to a series of consultation exercises, they became involved in developing proposals for the establishment of an out-of-hours helpline. Initially this service would be available only to selected carers and there were debates about the role of the Carers' Panel in defining and applying eligibility criteria (Barnes and Wistow 1994). Involvement in decision making about the allocation of services is obviously a rather different role from that of responding to proposals or expressing views about existing services, and not all carers felt comfortable about taking on this role. One of the conclusions from the Birmingham research was the need for clarity about roles and purposes and for negotiation about carers' wishes and expectations *vis-à-vis* those of the organisation sponsoring such an initiative.

What do carers want?

In this section we consider what has come from carer involvement in terms of the identification of issues of importance to carers. There is little evidence from research into carers' needs and experiences or from the campaigns of carers' organisations that families are seeking to give up their overall responsibilities for providing care and support (see, for example, Chamba *et al.* 1999; Nolan, Grant and Keady 1996; Walker and Warren 1996). What carers, and in some instances those receiving care, are asking for is emotional support and help with practical tasks from formal care providers. Requests for help and support may vary in frequency and type depending on individual circumstances and the problems experienced at a particular time. One of the outcomes of the evaluation of the Birmingham Community Care Special Action Project was the development of criteria which defined what carers considered to be a high-quality community service (see Barnes and Wistow 1993). See Box 6.1.

Box 6.1 Characteristics of a sensitive community care service

- Carers should be able to define their own needs.

- All services should be accessible from one point within the system: carers should not have to repeat their stories to different people as they get referred from one to another.

- Assessment of needs would lead to the relevant service being provided.

- Services would be provided immediately after the need has been identified and agreed.

- Choice of services, particularly respite care services, should be available in order to meet the different preferences and requirements of those admitted to care.

- Adaptations to homes should be carried out quickly, and there should be a follow up service in case things go wrong.

- Benefits should not be structured so that carers are penalised for encouraging independence.

- Benefits and other financial assistance should not assume that other family members will provide care (e.g. sitting time) free.

- Carers should be able to spend time talking about the effects on themselves of caring for a disabled relative or friend.

- Services should not be interrupted when people go on leave or change jobs.

- Home care services should recognise the importance to the self-esteem of elderly or disabled people of having a clean house and should provide a service which includes house cleaning.

- Service providers should negotiate with carers when home visits should take place.

- Carers should be confident that care provided outside the home is consistent with the quality of care which they provide.

- Carers need to be confident that service providers are planning future services to meet future needs.

Subsequent work with carers suggests that these criteria have not changed significantly. Yet recent studies suggest that, despite the implementation of the Carers (Recognition and Services) Act 1995 and the National Carers Strategy 1999, services are still not responding adequately to carers' needs.

There is evidence to suggest that a comprehensive or family-based approach to assessment and service provision is not widespread (Becker and Silburn 1999; SSI 1998) and that too much emphasis is given to the role of carers as resources rather than as co-workers (Twigg and Atkin 1994). The resulting problem for carers is that their needs, both within the caring relationship and outside of it, are understated.

For younger carers, the absence of a comprehensive assessment suggests that their psychological, emotional, educational and social needs go unrecognised, with the risk of potentially damaging consequences in later life (Becker and Silburn 1999). For carers who have responsibilities for family members other than the cared-for person, this oversight can lead to an often precarious balancing act between the demands of work, their own psychological well-being and providing care (Seddon 1999).

Tied into this is the apparent lack of timely and appropriate information. The need for information tends to fall into four main areas. First, access to user-friendly literature or discussions relating to prognosis and diagnosis, irrespective of whether the problem is a physical or mental health one. Understanding the progression of the illness or disability and the prospects for and the outcomes of treatment options are seen as a means through which carers can come to terms with a temporary or permanent incapacity of the cared-for person (Chamba *et al.* 1999; Rogers 2000). Second is information relating to emotional support, either through individual counselling or carers' groups. Accessing emotional support outside of a carer's established network is considered a safe way of exploring their anger, frustration, lost opportunities and possible guilt without appearing disloyal to the person they care for. Third, alongside the need for information about emotional support is the need for information about accessing financial advice. This takes the form of advice about state benefits but also includes the potential implications of moving from full-time to part-time work and the implications this type of decision may have on pension rights (Seddon 1999). Fourth, carers want information on the full range of services, in particular home-based care, short breaks and emergency respite, and on how these services can be accessed (Becker and Silburn 1999). But alongside carers' needs for information from paid workers, they also want workers to listen to and recognise the expertise and knowledge they have (Barnes 1997b; Nolan *et al.* 1996). For carers, as for service users, one of the main reasons for taking part in service decision making at both individual and collective levels is to ensure that their experiential knowledge is given equal weight to the professional knowledge of paid service providers.

Conclusion

The involvement of carers in decision making, either individually or collectively, reflects a broader trend towards participatory rights and responsibilities of citizenship and participatory democracy. Yet, as we have described, the good intentions contained within the rhetoric of central government are often hindered by insensitive implementation strategies that appear ignorant of carers' needs. Carers' needs have changed very little in the last twenty years but the unfortunate irony is that so too have service responses. If the relationship between service planners and providers and carers is to be effectively sustained, then this inertia needs to be addressed.

References

Abrams, P. (1985) 'Policies to promote informal care: Some reflections on voluntary action, neighbourhood involvement and neighbourhood care.' *Ageing and Society* 5, 1–18.

Archbold, P.G. (1983) 'Impact of parent-caring on women.' *Family Relations 32*, 39–45.

Arksey, H., Hepworth, D. and Qureshi, H. (2000) *Carers' Needs and the Carers Act: An Evaluation of the Process and Outcome of Assessment.* York: Social Policy Research Unit, University of York.

Atkin, K. (1991) 'Health, illness, disability and black minorities: A speculative critique of present day discourse.' *Disability, Handicap and Society 6*, 1, 37–47.

Barnes, M. (1997a) *Care, Communities and Citizens.* Harlow: Addison Wesley Longman Limited.

Barnes, M. (1997b) 'Families and empowerment.' In P. Ramcharan, G. Roberts, G. Grant and J. Borland (eds) *Empowerment in Everyday Life: Learning Disability.* London: Jessica Kingsley Publishers.

Barnes, M. (2002) 'From private carer to public actor: The Carers' Movement in England.' In M. Daly (ed) *Care Work Security and Representation.* Geneva: ILO.

Barnes, M. and Prior, D. (2000) *Private Lives as Public Policy.* Birmingham: Venture Press.

Barnes, M. and Wistow, G. (1992) *Coming in from the Wilderness? Carers' Views of the Consultations and their Outcomes.* BCCSAP Final Report 2, Nuffield Institute for Health, University of Leeds.

Barnes, M. and Wistow, G. (1993) *Gaining Influence, Gaining Support: Working with Carers in Research and Practice.* Leeds: Nuffield Institute for Health, University of Leeds.

Barnes, M. and Wistow, G. (1994) 'Involving carers in planning and review.' In A. Connor and S. Black (eds) *Performance Review and Quality in Social Care.* London: Jessica Kingsley Publishers.

Barnes, R.F., Raskind, M.A., Scott, M. and Murphy, C. (1981) 'Problems of families caring for Alzheimer patients: Use of a support group.' *Journal of the American Geriatrics Society 29*, 80–85.

Becker, S. (2000) 'Carers and indicators of vulnerability to social exclusion.' *Benefits 28*, 1–4, April/May.

Becker, S. and Silburn, R. (1999) *We're in this Together: Conversations with Families in Caring Relationships.* London: Carers National Association.

Booth, T. and Booth, W. (1994) *Parenting Under Pressure.* Buckingham: Open University Press.

Braithwaite, V.A. (1990) *Bound to Care.* Sydney: Allen and Unwin.

Braye, S. (2000) 'Participation and involvement in social care: An overview.' In H. Kemsall and R. Littlechild *User Involvement and Participation in Social Care. Research Informing Practice.* London: Jessica Kingsley Publishers.

Bulmer, M. (1987) *The Social Basis of Community Care.* London: Allen and Unwin.

Carers (Recognition and Services) Act (1995) London HMSO.

Chamba, R., Ahmad, W., Hirst, M., Lawton, D. and Beresford, B. (1999) *On the Edge: Minority Ethnic Families Caring for a Severely Disabled Child.* Bristol: The Policy Press.

Davis, A. Ellis, K. and Rummery, K. (1997) *Access to Assessment. Perspectives of Practitioners, Disabled People and Carers.* Bristol: The Policy Press.

DETR (Department of the Environment, Transport and the Regions) (1998) *Modern Government – In Touch with the People.* London: HMSO.

DETR (Department of the Environment, Transport and the Regions) (1999) *New Deal for Communities – An Overview.* London: DETR.

Dunkle, R. (1985) 'Comparing the depression of elders in two types of caregiving arrangements'. *Family Relations 34*, 235–240.

Ellis, K. (1993) *Squaring the Circle. User and Carer Participation in Needs Assessment.* York: Joseph Rowntree Foundation.

Frank, J., Tatum, C. and Tucker, S. (1999) *On Small Shoulders. Learning from the Experiences of Former Young Carers.* London: The Children's Society.

Grant, G. (1992) 'Researching user and carer involvement in mental handicap services.' In M. Barnes and G. Wistow (eds) *Researching User Involvement.* Leeds: Nuffield Institute for Health, University of Leeds.

Griffiths, R. (1988) *Community Care: Agenda for Action.* London: HMSO.

HM Government (1999) *Caring about Carers. A National Strategy for Carers.* London: The Stationery Office.

Hoyes, L., Jeffers, S., Lart, R., Means, R. and Taylor, M. (1993) *User Empowerment and the Reform of Community Care: An Interim Assessment.* Bristol: School for Advanced Urban Studies.

Humpreys. S. (1987) 'Participation in Practice'. *Social Policy and Administration 21*, 1, 28–39.

Lowndes, V., Pratchett, G. and Stoker, G. (1998) *Enhancing Public Participation in Local Government.* London: DETR.

McGrath, M. (1989) 'Consumer participation in service planning – the AWS Experience'. *Journal of Social Policy 18*, 1, 67–89.

McKenzie, H. (1995) 'Empowering older persons through organisations: A case study.' In D. Thursz, C. Nusberg and J. Prather (eds) *Empowering Older People.* London: Cassell.

National Health Service and Community Care Act (1990) London: HMSO.

Newton, B. and Becker, S. (1999) *The Capital Carers: An Evaluation of Capital Carers Young Carers Project.* Loughborough University, Young Carers Research Group.

Nolan, M., Grant, G. and Keady, J. (1996) *Understanding Family Care.* Buckingham: Open University Press.

Parker, G. (1990) *With Due Care and Attention: A Review of Research on Informal Care.* Buckingham: Open University Press.

Prior, D., Stewart, J. and Walsh, K. (1995) *Citizenship: Rights, Community and Participation.* London: Pitman.

Qureshi, H. and Walker, A. (1989) *The Caring Relationship: Elderly People and their Families.* Basingstoke: Macmillan.

Rogers, H. (2000) 'Breaking the ice: Developing strategies for collaborative working with carers of older people with mental health problems.' In H. Kemshall and R. Littlechild *User Involvement and Participation in Social Care. Research Informing Practice.* London: Jessica Kingsley Publishers.

Rummery, K. (2001) 'Community Care, Citizenship and Disability in the 1990s: Negotiating Needs and Access to Services.' PhD thesis, Department of Social Policy and Social Work, University of Birmingham.

Secretaries of State for Health, Social Security, Wales and Scotland (1989) *Caring for People: Community Care in the Next Decade and Beyond.* London: HMSO.

Seddon, D. (1999) 'Negotiating caregiving and employment.' In S. Cox and J. Keady *Younger People with Dementia. Planning, Practice and Development.* London: Jessica Kingsley Publishers.

SSI (Social Services Inspectorate) (1998) *A Matter of Chance for Carers.* London: Department of Health.

Thomas, C. (1993) 'De-constructing concepts of care.' *Sociology 27,* 4, 649–669.

Twigg, J., Atkin, K. and Perring, C. (1990) *Carers and Services: A Review of Research.* London: HMSO.

Twigg, J. and Atkin, K. (1994) *Carers Perceived. Policy and Practice in Informal Care.* Buckingham: Open University Press.

Ungerson, C. (1987) *Policy is Personal: Sex, Gender and Informal Care.* London: Tavistock.

Walker, A. (1982) (ed) *Community Care: The Family, the State and Social Policy.* Oxford: Blackwell and Robertson.

Walker, A. and Warren, L. (1996) *Changing Services for Older People.* Buckingham: Open University Press.

CHAPTER 7

Carers and Employment

Paul Ramcharan and Bridget Whittell

Introduction

A recent report, commissioned by Carers UK, predicts that amongst the population aged 45–64, there is currently a 9.9 per cent chance of becoming a carer in any one year, with demographic changes increasing this likelihood to almost 15 per cent by the year 2037 (George 2001). According to the Government's National Strategy for Carers, some 49 per cent of the present estimated total of 5.7 million carers (looking after family members or friends who are sick, disabled, vulnerable or frail) in Great Britain are working, either full or part time, while a further 26 per cent are retired. The remaining 25 per cent of carers are either unemployed or economically inactive. This includes those carers unable to work because of the nature of their caring responsibilities (Department of Health 1999, p.17). The financial cost of caring can itself be high (Crossroads 1993; Dobson and Middleton 1998; Holzhausen and Pearlman 2000) leaving families in a financially precarious position. And, although unemployed carers are not a homogeneous group, several studies point to significant numbers who would work if they could (Caring Costs Alliance 1996; Kagan, Lewis and Heaton 1997; Lankshear, Giarchi and Cox 2000; McLaughlin and Ritchie 1994).

This chapter seeks to examine more closely the nature and experience of several groups of carers: those leaving or reducing employment to care; those balancing their work and care responsibilities; and those who wish to (re-)enter employment. Consideration of these areas is prefaced by a consideration of the present policy position in relation to employment and care, allowing us in making our concluding remarks to ask how policy might best be restructured to support carers in their employment aspirations. Arguments will be made for the need to rethink the focus of policy. In particular, we will ask whether policies and initiatives based on partnership can or should be relocated within an employment policy framework.

Carers and employment: the official response

Until relatively recently, carer employment issues have seldom featured in policy or practice guidance documents although, as Hirst (2001) has commented, supporting carers is a rapidly evolving policy arena. Significant amongst recent policy initiatives have been the Carers (Recognition and Services) Act 1995 (DoH 1995), Caring About Carers: A National Strategy for Carers (DoH 1999) and, more recently, the Carers and Disabled Children Act 2000 (DoH 2001). One might argue that these policies emphasise supporting carers to continue in their caring role. The National Strategy for Carers (DoH 1999) devotes a whole chapter to carers and employment. Within the Strategy, the Government states that its objectives for working-age carers are: 'to encourage and enable carers to remain in work; to help those carers who are unable to, or do not want to, combine paid work with caring to return to work *when their caring responsibilities cease*' (our emphasis) (DoH 1999, p.27). However, there is no mention of support for carers who want to combine paid work with caring but who are not working, including those who have had to give up work to care. Instead, there is an emphasis on supporting carers who are already working via the development of flexible employment practices and carer-friendly employment policies (see Table 7.1, p.150). Flexible employment practices and family friendly policies are aimed at benefiting all employees, not just carers, and we would argue that the focus is on mainstream caring responsibilities, that is, ordinary childcare and possibly eldercare. The government's proposals for developing these flexible employment practices and family-friendly policies are contained in the White Paper, *Fairness at Work* (Department of Trade and Industry 1998) and the Work-Life Balance campaign launched in Spring 2000 (Department for Education and Employment 2000).

Even where initiatives that specifically mention carers can be identified, their needs in relation to employment are not fully acknowledged or recognised. For example, the White Paper *Modernising Social Services* (DoH 1998) identifies a responsibility for local authorities to ensure that services are provided in ways that maximise both service users' and carers' capacity to work. However, a Social Services Inspectorate report reviewing the progress of eight councils in 2000 found that supporting disabled people and their carers into employment was not a priority area for them (Griffiths 2001).

There are some encouraging signs, however, that carers are at last becoming more visible in the area of employment, with a number of pilot projects being implemented. For example, Lankshear *et al.* (2000) report the findings of an innovative project called 'Caring Options for Training and Work'. Part funded by the European Social Fund, the project was about developing a model that would assist local carers to access a range of information on training and work opportunities. The project took place in Devon and Surrey and had European partners in Italy, France, Belgium and Spain. Recently, substantial funding from the European Social Fund's EQUAL programme has been secured for a three-year project called Action for Carers into Employment (ACE). This large, national project involves a number of partners across the UK including carers' organisations, employers, unions, training and service providers 'to work with relevant agencies to test the mechanisms that will enable carers across all disadvantaged groups to overcome the multiple barriers to employment that they face' (ACE National Partnership 2002).

Despite such innovative initiatives, government-led policy remains focused on mainstream carers, with the emphasis on providing support to those carers who are already working. It is possible that Hirst's observation that government policy is about supporting carers may be recouched in terms of the notion of 'the gift' (Gavron 1966), that is, providing support to carers to remain carers. Where policies do exist for carers not in work they pay most attention to the person being cared for (for example, joint investment plans for welfare to work for disabled people) or the needs of the perceived mainstream. If the interest of family carers is to be addressed it is therefore necessary to look more closely at their experience in relation to employment issues.

Much of the literature on carers and employment to date has tended to focus attention on those carers already in employment. It is our view that a thorough understanding of employment and caring is served by understanding other experiences including, for example, those of unemployed carers and those who have given up or reduced their employment to care, or those wishing to work and to seek employment. Figure 7.1 below provides an heuristic for reviewing our current knowledge and the boxes provide a focus for each of the following sections.

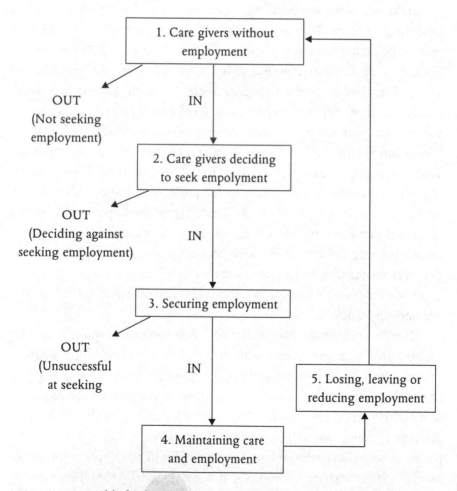

Figure 7.1 A Mondel of Seeking Work and Maintaining Work and Care

Care givers without employment: the carer career

Many carers find themselves making the decision to leave or reduce employment because of their commitment to providing (more) care (Figure 7.1: Boxes 5 and 1 respectively). Because of this it has been found that carers are less likely to be in full-time employment than non-carers (Evandrou 1995, p.22) and that 'co-resident carers' (that is, those providing care for someone in their own home) are twice as likely to have reduced work hours or to have left work than the population as a whole (Corti *et al.* 1994). Many carers have either lost or given up work so that they can provide care (Box 1, Figure 7.1) and this applies disproportionately to women (Beresford 1995; Shearn 1998; Shearn and Todd 2000). In a study of 'mid-life women' in work, 20 per cent ($n = 77$) were found to be considering quitting work to care (Gibeau *et al.* 1987) and up to one-third of women found that caring responsibilities meant giving up work (Wright 1986).

Studies of the employment patterns of carers have variously shown that:

- parents of children with disabilities have been found less likely to be in employment and to have lower earnings than other parents (Baldwin 1985; Parker and Lawton 1990)

- nearly a fifth of women carers reported lowered employment prospects (Corti *et al.* 1994; Martin and Roberts 1984)

- towards the end of their working lives, third-age carers had spent less time in employment than non-carers (Askham *et al.* 1992)

- early retirement for 'family reasons' is also common though more likely amongst women than men in their fifties (Laczko and Phillipson 1991).

Particularly for those who are out of work there is a high economic cost. One estimate for female carers having given up work suggests a £7000–8000 per annum loss of income (Joshi 1987). In a study of thirty carers, financial burdens were found to be most acute for single carers not in full-time employment (Glendinning 1988).

As pointed out by many writers, however, the costs are not only associated with loss of employment income. In a survey of carers and non-carers in the workforce, it was found that 14 per cent of carers had contributed to the cost of looking after dependants, 63 per cent spending up to £20 a week (Crossroads 1993, p.17) and receiving less than adequate social security benefits. It is likely that for those not in employment such financial burdens will be even more crippling. Loss of pension rights for those who have been out of employment due to caring responsibilities are therefore also significant losses of income.

And, when caring comes to an end, there have also been indications that the effects of providing care over the long term are characterised by anxiety, stress, loss of confidence and self-esteem, and difficulties renewing 'fractured social networks' (McLaughlin and Ritchie 1994). The long-term consequences were found to be most deleterious for those providing care for more disabled relatives, those with care duties of over fifty hours per week and those who had cared for a number of years. Moreover, 'Carers who had continued to work had better options for employment after caring had ended' (McLaughlin and Ritchie 1994, p.251).

Wanting to work and seeking to secure employment

Beyond the obvious benefits of economic well-being, relatively little is documented about the motives carers have for wanting to move back into the workplace, that is, why they decide to seek work (Box 2, Figure 7.1). There is therefore no literature on the 'push' factors that prompt carers back into the workplace. Similarly, the literature only fleetingly considers the actual process of carers seeking to secure employment, the methods that they use, the difficulties that they encounter and the outcomes of their efforts (Box 3, Figure 7.1).

It has been reported that, in seeking to find work, only 38 per cent of carers knew a voluntary organisation that might help, only 4 per cent used respite, 33 per cent had not even heard of respite care and there was confusion among carers over welfare benefits (Crossroads 1993). The Crossroads report also found that one-third of respondents did not know who to turn to for advice in relation to caring, and that while social services have a responsibility for advising carers, only 38 per cent would turn to them for help, 25 per cent to GPs and 11 per cent to the CAB or DSS. Very few mentioned employers themselves as a source of help and advice, highlighting the lack of partnership between the employment and care sectors. The report argues that there is an 'expectation gap' in care provision suggesting the need for 'a public education campaign to help people become more aware of the services and benefits on offer to carers' (Crossroads 1993, p.4).

Studies also variously show difficulties in moving back into employment. Early studies point to the 'daily grind', school holidays, bouts of illness or regular hospital appointments, job restrictions and lack of employer understanding as reasons for carers not seeking work (Glendinning 1983). Other difficulties highlighted include concerns over respite, financial constraints, lack of time, lack of confidence, lack of experience, age, concerns for their own and the cared-for person's health, perceived employer discrimination against carers and a lack of available jobs (Lankshear, Giarchi and Cox 2000). In addition, others point to few locally based jobs suiting their care requirements, and a lack of alternative day care or substitute care (Kagan *et al.* 1998), lost skills (Chwarae Teg and CNA undated), inappropriately targeted training (Pearson 1994), much greater difficulties for those caring for persons with higher support needs (Booth and Kelly 1999), greater difficulties for disabled carers (Brandon 2000), slowness of services to respond when work becomes available (Contact a Family 1994) and substitute costs that often made working less than worthwhile (European Fund 1996).

The heterogeneity of carers means that though they may experience common difficulties they will also face specific problems according to their individual circumstances and caring situations. In this light there are also a number of positive reasons for carers seeking work. It has been found that carers often wish to develop their 'carer only' self-identity and to fulfil personal ambitions through employment (Chamberlayne and King 1997; Todd and Shearn 1996). In wanting to combine work and care, psychological reasons or self-development motivations appear to be more important to carers than purely financial incentive. Early findings from the Advocating for Work and Care project (Whittell and Ramcharan 2000) in which the two authors of this chapter are presently involved, have mirrored many of the above findings. These findings demonstrate the wide range of positions carers take in relation to work and a complex of factors relevant to their decision to seek work in the first place. As well as diverse caring contexts it is equally important to remember that the life situation of individual carers is not static.

This diversity and situational change has been a critical issue in the findings of the Advocating for Work and Care study in relation to carers thinking about returning to employment. Very small changes in the caring situation, recurrent crises and the demands of other (dependent) family members, among other things, are likely to have a substantial impact on a carer's pattern of responsibility. This in turn can easily affect their motivation as well as the practicality of seeking work. Faced with a care service that cannot act at the drop of a hat when work is found, the timetables of the professional and the familial care world are rendered asynchronous. If relative stability is a prior condition to (wishing to find) work, then the conditions under which carers make their decisions about work do not lend themselves to this pursuit. Moreover, because under such conditions carers have no control over situations, stress is a likely product. Since the 'conditions of caring' are often not in the control of the carer, remedies need to be manufactured that can counteract this problem (Shearn and Todd 2000).

The problems of finding work can be exacerbated by present community care policy (DoH 1989). The NHS and Community Care Act 1990 drew a great deal on pilot studies that sought to balance formal statutory service provision with informal sources of care (Challis and Davies 1986). It was also the aim of community care policy to provide care in homes and homely environments. There is an issue here about the extent to which family carers can sustain care in the home before seeking alternatives, despite their own or their relative's wishes. There may, therefore, be a perverse incentive built in to the present community care legislation that penalises carers and their relatives if the carer decides to seek work. Moreover, with cost ceilings on care packages and financial assessments also necessary (Grant *et al.* 1997), it may be that carers will be put off looking for work because it simply does not pay to do so.

It has been posited that inflexible employer practices and, one might add, entering employment

> would lead to increases in demand for community care services and, ultimately, hospital and nursing home care. If these services are not forthcom-

ing, one might further expect an increase in the use of health services...as stress...affects both psychological and physical health (Gilhooly and Redpath 1997, p.407).

The cost equation for the public purse is therefore complex. Seeking work whilst caring represents a major challenge for some carers and, as will be suggested later, may be a function of the organisation of social policy initiatives that effectively work to keep carers in their caring role.

Maintaining work and care

Despite the difficulties involved, it is estimated that nearly a half of all carers (DoH 1999) combine work with caring (Box 4, Figure 7.1) and that between 15 and 25 per cent of employees combine a work and care-giving role (Gilhooly and Redpath 1997). Other data suggest that of those carers spending at least twenty hours a week caring, 43 per cent of working age had some paid employment, 26 per cent full time and 17 per cent part time (Green 1988). A more recent review of the data in the 1991 British Household Panel Survey found that for co-resident carers 44 per cent of men, 37 per cent of non-married women and 17 per cent of married women were in full-time work. These figures are substantially lower than for the population as a whole, where 60 per cent of men, 46 per cent of non-married women and 28 per cent of married women were in full-time work. A similar difference was found in relation to those in part-time work (Corti *et al.* 1994, p.31).

In Britain, much of the work in relation to employer practices that has arisen in the last decade or so draws on a longer US tradition in this area (Creedon 1995). Reviewing recent initiatives in the workplace, Phillips (1995) reports that limited eldercare initiatives have been located in large companies in the 1990s (Institute of Personnel Management 1990) and there have only been limited developments in Europe (Hoffman and Leeson,1994). These large companies are more likely to have carer policies and offer flexibility in the form of long-term time off without pay, leave of absence with job security, geographical transfer and moves to part-time working (see Table 7.1). However, for the majority of employees there remains a lack of flexibility and understanding from employers (Kagan *et al.*

1998). In a postal questionnaire to companies drawn from the register of the Scottish Chamber of Commerce it is reported that 92 per cent of private sector companies had never considered employees' eldercare responsibilities as an issue (Gilhooly and Redpath 1997) and, whilst sympathetic, were not responsive.

While there seems evidence that the public sector is adopting flexible working practices (Naegele and Reichert 1995), how these are benefiting employees with caring responsibilities remains to be studied. Findings from the Work Life Balance Baseline Study carried out in 2000 indicate 'clear evidence of a substantial and unsatisfied demand amongst lone parents, carers and disabled people', suggesting that some of the flexible working practices being introduced fall short of those actually needed, with demand amongst carers suggesting a 'preference for part-time hours and flexitime as well as a compressed working week' (Hogarth et al. 2000 p.37). Furthermore, there remains a suspicion that not only are larger companies more able to absorb the requirements of employee flexibility but that since these are likely to involve the 'white-collar' workforce, it may further disadvantage the 'blue-collar' workforce or occupations involving manual labour. As such, recent initiatives calling for company audits and policies on flexibility, such as Carers in Employment (The Princess Royal Trust for Carers 1995), Fair Play in Merseyside (CEWTEC Ltd et al. 1997) and Work Life Balance (DTI 2001), may, if adopted by larger companies alone, provide solutions for only the minority of carers.

As with unemployed carers, there is evidence that those in employment are economically disadvantaged, fail to realise their full potential (Evandrou 1995), work below their skill capacity (Glendinning 1988; Kagan *et al.* 1998), fail to take up training opportunities (Seddon 1999) and have reduced chances for promotion (Crossroads 1993). The General Household Survey (OPCS 1992) indicates that men caring for a dependant inside the household averaged an hourly wage rate of £6.40, those providing over fifty hours care earned £5.48, while non-carers got £7.26. A similar pattern, though less extreme, applies to women (Evandrou 1995, p.31). All of these contribute to difficulties across the life course once care has started (Hancock *et al.* 1995).

Once again, and like unemployed carers, less income is not the only negative effect. It has been variously reported that 40 per cent of carers take time off to look after relatives (Berry-Lound 1994), up to 8.8 hours average per month according to some estimates (Scharlach 1994). Caring is characterised by lost leisure and social relationships (Naegele and Reichert 1995); carers show a lack of energy arising from rearranging schedules, using vacations and sick leave to provide care (European Foundation 1996; Phillips 1995); and effectiveness at work has been reduced (Crossroads 1993). At work they also show tiredness, apathy, lack of concentration and, at the same time, guilt (Berry-Lound 1994) and, ultimately, often keep their caring responsibilities hidden from employers (Whatmore 1989). Many carers seek to accommodate these difficulties by taking part-time jobs or, where there are children, jobs that provide time off during school holidays. They thus become 'long-term marginal workers' (Glendinning 1983).

Balancing the work/caring interface is an extremely difficult process. It is not facilitated by the fact that statutory services do not stretch to supporting people in employment (Parker and Lawton 1990). As Phillips (1995) notes, 'little attention has been paid to the role of employers in the discussion of community care' (p.55). More will be said of this in our concluding remarks. For now it is sufficient to note that the experiences of carers seeking to balance work and care can present a tough juggling act. There have been some outstanding small-scale studies which incorporate experiences of balancing work and care giving (Baldwin 1985; Glendinning 1992; Parker 1993; Phillips 1993), though more recently this experience has been placed within three models.

According to the 'compensatory model', benefits for care givers in combining both roles are developing a social (support) network, reducing isolation and acting as a 'stress buffer' (Chwarae Teg and CNA undated; Shearn and Todd 2000; Staines 1980). Further benefits reported are a respite function (Neal *et al.* 1990), satisfying monetary needs, contributing to self-confidence and motivation (Commission for European Communities 1994), economic and psychological benefit for those being cared for (Kagan, Lewis and Heaton 1998), bringing interpersonal and management skills from the caring role to their work roles (Laczko and Noden 1992) and, where supported, being both loyal to the company and enhancing the company image (European Foundation 1996).

In opposition to the compensatory model others have argued for a 'role conflict' model (Murphy *et al.* 1997; Stull *et al.* 1994), based upon balancing differing roles (work, family, caring) and characterised by higher levels of stress (Brody *et al.* 1987; Creedon, 1987; Gibeau and Anastas 1989; Harper and Lund 1990; Kendig 1983). Indicators of role conflict might be work interruptions, less energy and unpaid leave and these are more likely to be experienced where the dependant's level of impairment is higher (Lechner 1993; Scharlach *et al.* 1991). Moreover, combining such roles is also indicated to have negative effects on health (Brody *et al.* 1987; Creedon 1987; Murphy *et al.* 1997; Scharlach *et al.* 1991) and physical and psychological effects (Lewis and Meredith 1988; McLaughlin and Ritchie 1994).

More recently, in the wider literature on work–life balance, the importance of balancing different life commitments and roles has been highlighted in the 'quality of life' model that has seemingly replaced the theoretical division between proponents of the 'role conflict' versus 'compensatory' models. In this approach it is possible to find a balance between differing demands with a view to maximising the quality of life of carers, those for whom they care and families. This literature has yet to produce the empirical substantiation of its theory but is based on a series of studies showing that those balancing work and care among their commitments tend to experience the deleterious effects of caring to a lesser degree (Lewis 1996; Moen *et al.* 1995; Stephens *et al.* 1994, 1997). Indeed, Marks (1994) goes so far as to argue that a balance between different commitments is better than either under- or over-commitment to any one role. It has also been found that physical and emotional indicators were less deleterious where carers expressed satisfactions with both their caring and work roles (Martire *et al.* 1997; Warfield 2001). This has relevance not only in relation to those in employment, but to those who maintain a role as carer without being in paid work, more particularly for those who would, if possible, enter employment. It might be hypothesised from this literature on workplace stress that 'being in control' of circumstances and conditions around employment represents a vital component in mitigating the effect of balancing commitments. This fact underscores the importance of employer-friendly policies that can provide the right and legitimacy to carers making choices to sustain the work–life balance (see Figure 7.1).

However, this still leaves open the question of who should shoulder the additional costs of maintaining carers in work. Family- and carer-friendly policies have been taken up by few companies and largely those of sufficient size to absorb immediate costs. It has, however, been argued that family-friendly policies lead to staff retention, higher productivity and skills (Chwarae Teg and CNA, undated), though, at the end of the day 'For organisations the ultimate focus is on work outcomes ...that they contribute to workers being at work and working productively' (Raabe 1996, p.129).

While there is nothing intrinsically problematic about role conflict studies, nor other studies outlined above, there seem to be some important omissions. It has been pointed out that 'role theory' considers the problems and benefits only from the carer's point of view. There is, therefore, a need to examine issues relating to families (Russell 1994), to the persons being cared for (Keith and Morris 1996), and to relationships and reciprocities within family life and familial negotiation (Finch and Mason 1993), though space does not permit a consideration of these here. In addition, there are very little data available about how the stresses and satisfactions of caring change as circumstances change. Nor is there any longitudinal data set looking at how coping and management strategies for caring change as do situations. Combining the elements of stress, satisfaction, and coping and management strategies (Nolan *et al.* 1997) within a family systems dynamic may further contribute to knowledge in this area.

A substantial number of recommendations have been generated from the studies of balancing work and care, many of which have been mentioned in this chapter. These recommendations are summarised in Table 7.1 on the following page.

Table 7.1: Outlining recommendations relating to balancing work and care and relevant texts citing these recommendations

Area of recommendation	*Recommendation*	*Cited in*
Employer issues: 1. Flexibility	Employer flexibility	DTI 1998; DfEE 2000; Kagan, Lewis and Heaton 1997; Naergele and Reichert 1995; Seddon 1999
	Company policy required/ commitment of management	CEWTEC *et al.* 1997
2. Emergency time off	Emergency days off/ flexible leave/time off for relevant appointments	CEWTEC *et al.* 1997; Chwarae Teg and CNA (n.d.); European Foundation 1996; Gilhooly and Redpath 1997
3. Contractual arrangements	Flexitime Lower working hours Compressed working week Sell leisure to buy days off Job sharing Homeworking/teleworking Consortia of companies to spread cost	Kagan *et al.* 1998 Chwarae Teg and CNA (n.d.) European Foundation 1996
Replacement care dimension	Daycare in the workplace Better childcare	Ameghino 1998; Axtell *et al.* 1995; Booth and Kelly 1999; Bailey *et al.* 1992; Freedman *et al.* 1995; Hoskins 1994; Kagan *et al.* 1998
	Subsidised day services	European Foundation 1996

Service and support dimension	Direct support service for working carers and families	Axtell *et al.* 1995; Bailey *et al.* 1992; Kagan *et al.* 1998; Booth and Kelly 1999; Freedman *et al.*; Hoskins 1994
	Improved information to carers, e.g. benefits	Anastob, Gibeau and Larson 1990;
	Better co-ordination between services and employers	Kagan *et al.* 1998
	More flexible appointment times outside of hours	Kagan *et al.* 1998
		Kagan *et al.* 1998
Government and wider	Tax allowance or tax credits Care allowance Re-examination of pensions/social security Tactical role for unions Lobbying role for NGOs Awareness raising Meeting ILO conventions	European Foundation 1996; Loeis 1996.
	Working time account/career break system	Moss 1996
	Better funding for community care provision	Kagan *et al.* 1998

Policy, employment and caring: some concluding remarks

Where policy and practice recommendations have been made, the majority of the literature reviewed above tends to focus recommendations within the domain of those who are seeking to balance work and care. By doing so there is an implicit acceptance of the system as it presently exists. Despite contemporary partnership policies between employment and care responsibilities, reviewed in the introduction to this chapter, there still seems to be an emphasis within social policy on maintaining carers in their caring role. As Chamberlayne and King (2000) argue, 'increased reliance on the informal sphere is the corollary to welfare retrenchment' (p.9). Once the carer has left employment most policy makes mention of their employment rights only once caring has come to an end. In this sense such carers are, by virtue of the policy emphasis, living in an 'invisible world' in relation to employment. They are likely to remain 'unseen' within the private home sphere, a point of particular relevance to women and their participation and citizenship rights (Lister 1990). Policies of partnership are largely fractured at this point.

Nor is it necessarily the case that those being cared for would wish their carer to give up work to provide their care. One study, for example, showed that, among older people being cared for, over half felt that their daughters should not be prepared to give up work to care for them (Kozak 1998). There is an important principle here about giving people the choice not to have to make their life decisions based purely on constraint and, moreover, maximising the potential economic productivity of the nation. Yet at present the social policy emphasis remains squarely within the domain of extending 'social capital', that is, 'the capacity to mobilize support and resources in the informal sphere, based on norms of reciprocity and networks of civic engagement' (Chamberlayne and King 2000, p.9). Ultimately, though, social capital will not be sufficient on its own. Supporting people to work despite the conditions that constrain their involvement in the labour market will also be based upon the ability of care services to meet the needs of those being cared for whilst maintaining them in 'homes and homely environments'. At present levels of funding this is likely to remain highly problematic.

More importantly, where there is a need for flexible employment policy to allow people to balance work and care responsibilities, then who should shoulder the costs? Up to now carers have largely themselves carried the burden of costs for caring, and remain a largely unpaid workforce doubly disadvantaged by care costs and reduced or no employment income. 'Additional research is needed to review the costs to employers of eldercare programmes as well as the benefits of community partnerships in the provision of such benefits… However without adequate community services …[carers] will have to take time off work' (Singleton 2000, p.374).

Perhaps, if employment is an important key to self-accomplishment and maximising the quality of life of families, the solutions should *not* be placed within social care or social policy domains, both of which marginalise people. An alternative would be to make the leading policy area that of employment. This might involve partnering employment with social security, that is, a system of 'flexicurity' allowing access to benefits whilst carers remain in work. It may also involve additional taxation, a social care stamp or insurance against the eventuality of caring likely to be experienced by a growing number of people in the years to come. But the spectre of increased taxation remains perhaps the most politically sensitive of areas and one that governments are loathe to advocate.

The issue of carers and employment, however, is becoming more visible. If there is a serious intent behind government policy to respond appropriately and effectively, then, as indicated at the beginning of this chapter, demographic projections alone suggest this is an area requiring a radical rethink in the immediate future.

References

ACE National Partnership (2002) *Partnership Agreement.* London: Carers UK.

Ameghino, J. (1998) 'Creche Landing.' *Guardian,* Wednesday August 26.

Anastas, J.W., Gibeau, J.L. and Larson, P.J. (1990) 'Working families and eldercare: A national perspective in an aging America.' *Social Work 35*, 5, 405–411.

Askham, J., Grundy, E. and Tinker, A. (1992) *Caring: The Importance of Third Age Carers.* The Carnegie Inquiry into the Third Age, Research Paper No.6. Fife: The Carnegie Trust.

Axtell, S., Garwick, A., Patterson, J., Bennett, F. and Blum, R. (1995) 'Unmet service needs of families of young children with chronic illness and disabilities.' *American Journal on Mental Retardation 16*, 395–411.

Bailey, D., Blasco, P. and Simeonsson, R. (1992) 'Needs expressed by mothers and fathers of young children with disabilities.' *Family in Society: Journal of Contemporary Human Services 76*, 507–514.

Baldwin, S. (1985) *The Costs of Caring: Families with Disabled Children.* London: Routledge & Kegan Paul.

Beresford, B. (1995) *Expert Opinions: A National Survey of Parents Caring for a Severely Disabled Child.* Bristol: Policy Press.

Berry-Lound, D. (1994) *Help the Aged Seniorcare Survey.* London: Help the Aged.

Booth, C.L. and Kelly, J.F. (1999) 'Child care and employment in relation to infants' disabilities and risk factors.' *American Journal on Mental Retardation 104*, 117–130.

Brandon, P.D. (2000) 'Child care utilisation among working mothers raising children with disabilities.' *Journal of Family and Economic Issues 21*, 4, 343–363.

Brody, E.M., Kleban, M.H., Johnsen, P., Hoffman, C. and Shoonover, C. (1987) 'Work status and parent care: A comparison of four groups of women.' *The Gerontologist 27*, 201–208.

Caring Costs Alliance (1996) *The True Cost of Caring: A Survey of Carers' Lost Income.* London: Caring Costs Alliance.

CEWTEC Ltd., Merseyside TEC Ltd., St.Helens Chambers of Commerce Training and Enterprise and the European Social Fund (1997) *Fair Play Merseyside: Family Friendly Policies: Good Practice Guide.* Liverpool: Fair Play Merseyside.

Challis, D. and Davies, B. (1986) *Care Management in Community Care.* Aldershot: Gower.

Chamberlayne, P. and King, A. (1997) 'The biographical challenge of caring.' *The Sociology of Health and Illness 5*, 580–601.

Chamberlayne, P. and King, A. (2000) *Cultures of Care: Biographies of Carers in Britain and the two Germanies.* Bristol: The Policy Press.

Chwarae Teg and CNA (undated) *Flexible Work Practices.* Cardiff: Chwarae Teg.

Commission for European Communities (1994) *European Social Policy – A Way Forward for the Union.* White Paper. Brussels: EEC.

Contact a Family (1994) *Working and Parenting.* London: Contact a Family.

Corti, L., Laurie, H. and Dex, S. (1994) *Caring and Employment.* ESRC Research Centre on Micro-social Change, Department of Employment Research Series No.39, University of Essex.

Creedon, M.A. (1987) *Issues for an Aging America: Employees and Eldercare.* Bridgeport CT: Centre for the Study of Aging.

Creedon, M. (1995) 'Eldercare and work research in the United States.' In J. Phillips (ed) *Working Carers.* Aldershot: Avebury.

Crossroads (1993) *Looking Forward to Looking After.* London: Crossroads.

DfEE (Department for Education and Employment) (2000) *Work–Life Balance: Changing Patterns in a Changing World.* London: Department for Education and Employment.

DoH (Department of Health) (1989) *Caring for People in the Next Decade and Beyond.* Cm 849. London: HMSO.

DoH (Department of Health) (1995) Carers (Recognition and Services) Act. London: HMSO.

DoH (Department of Health) (1998) *Modernising Social Services – Promoting Independence, Improving Protection, Raising Standards.* London: HMSO.

DoH (Department of Health) (1999) *Caring About Carers: A National Strategy for Carers.* London: The Stationery Office.

DoH (Department of Health) (2001) *Carers and Disabled Children Act 2000.* London: HMSO.

DTI (Department of Trade and Industry) (1998) *Fairness at Work*. Cm 3968. London: Department of Trade and Industry.

DTI (Department of Trade and Industry) (2001) *Work Life Balance: The Business Case*. London: Department of Trade and Industry.

Dobson, B. and Middleton, S. (1998) *Paying to Care: The Cost of Childhood Disability*. York: Joseph Rowntree Foundation.

European Foundation for the Improvement of Living and Working Conditions (1996) *Working and Caring: Developments at the Workplace for Family Carers of Disabled and Older People*. Dublin: European Foundation for the Improvement of Living and Working Conditions.

Evandrou, M. (1995) 'Employment and care, paid and unpaid work: The socio-economic position of informal carers in Britain.' In J. Phillips (ed) *Working Carers*. Aldershot: Avebury.

Finch, J. and Mason, J. (1993) *Negotiating Family Responsibilities*. London: Routledge.

Freedman, R., Litchfield, L., and Warfield, M.E. (1995) 'Balancing work and family responsibilities.' *Families in Society: Journal of Contemporary Human Services 76*, 507–514.

Gavron, H. (1966) *The Captive Wife: Conflicts of Housebound Mothers*. London: Routledge & Kegan Paul.

George, M. (2001) *...It could be you: A report on the chances of becoming a carer*. London: Carers UK.

Gibeau, J.L. and Anastas, J.W. (1989) 'Breadwinners and caregivers: Interviews with working women.' *Journal of Gerontological Social Work 14*, 1/2, 19–40.

Gibeau, J.L., Anastas, J.W. and Larson, P. (1987) *Breadwinners and Caregivers: Supporting Workers who Care for Elderly Family Members*. Final report submitted by the National Association of Area Agencies on Ageing to the Administration on Ageing, Washington DC.

Gilhooly, M.L. and Redpath, C. (1997) 'Private sector policies for caregiving employees: A survey of Scottish companies.' *Ageing and Society 17*, 399–423.

Glendinning, C. (1983) *Unshared Care: Parents and their Disabled Children*. London: Routledge & Kegan Paul.

Glendinning, C. (1988) 'Dependency and interdependency: The incomes of informal carers and the impact of social security.' In R. Walker (ed) *Social Security and Community Care*. Aldershot: Avebury.

Glendinning, C. (1992) *The Costs of Informal Care: Looking inside the household*. London: HMSO.

Grant, G., Parry-Jones, B., Ramcharan, P. and Robinson, C. (1997) *The Practitioner's Voice: Assessment and Care Management in Wales*. Bangor: Centre for Social Policy Research and Development.

Green, H. (1988) *Informal Carers*. General Household Survey 1985, Series GH5, No. 25 Supplement A. London: HMSO.

Griffiths, G. (2001) *Making it Work: Inspection of Welfare to Work for Disabled People.* London: Department of Health.

Hancock, R., Jarvis, C., Tinker, A. and Askham, J. (1995) *After Care.* London: Age Concern, Baring Foundation.

Harper, S. and Lund, D.A. (1990) 'Wives, husbands and daughters caring for institutionalised and non-institutionalised dementia patients: Towards a model of caregiver burden.' *International Journal of Aging and Human Development 304,* 241–262.

Hirst, M. (2001) 'Trends in informal care in Great Britain during the 1990s.' *Health and Social Care in the Community 9,* 6, 348–357.

Hoffman, M. and Leeson, G. (1994) *Eldercare and Employment: Workplace Policies and Initiatives to Support Workers who are Carers.* Dublin: Report for the European Foundation for the Improvement of Living and Working Conditions.

Hogarth, T., Hasluck, C. and Pierre, G. with Winterbotham, M. and Vivan, D. (2000) *Work–Life Balance 2000: Baseline Study of Work–life Balance Practices in Great Britain, Summary Report.* London: Department for Education and Employment.

Holzhausen, E. and Pearlman, V. (2000) *Caring on the Breadline – the Financial Implications of Caring.* London: Carers National Association.

Hoskins, I. (1994) 'Working women and eldercare: A six-nation overview.' *Ageing International,* June, 58–62.

Institute of Personnel Management (1990) *Work and the Family: Carer Friendly Employment Practice.* London: IPM.

Joshi, H. (1987) 'The cost of caring.' In C. Glendinning and J. Millar (eds) *Women and Poverty in Britain.* Hemel Hempstead: Harvester Wheatsheaf.

Kagan, C., Lewis, S. and Heaton, P. (1997) 'The context of work and caring for parents of disabled children.' Manchester: Interpersonal Organisational Development Research Group, Manchester Metropolitan University. IOD Occasional paper: number 1/97.

Kagan, C., Lewis, S. and Heaton, P. (1998) *Caring to Work: Accounts of Working Parents of Disabled Children.* London: Family Policy Studies Centre in association with the Joseph Rowntree Foundation.

Keith, L. and Morris, J. (1996) 'Easy targets: A disability rights perspective on the "children as carers" debate.' In J. Morris (ed) *Encounters with Strangers.* London: The Women's Press.

Kendig, H. (1983) *Blood Ties and Gender Roles: Adult Children who Care for Aged Parents.* Support Networks, 5. Melbourne: Institute of Family Studies.

Korodinski, J. and Shirey, L. (2000) 'The impact of living with an elder parent on adult daughter's labour supply and hours of work.' *Journal of Family and Economic Issues 21,* 2, 149–175.

Kozak, M. (1998) *Employment, Family Life and the Quality of Care Services: A Review of Research in the UK.* London: Department for Education and Employment. Research Report RR54.

Laczko, F. and Noden, S. (1992) 'Eldercare and the labour market: Combining care and work.' In Laczko, F. and Victor, C.R. *Social Policy and Elderly People: The Role of Community Care.* Avebury: Aldershot.

Laczko, F. and Phillipson, C. (1991) *Changing Work and Retirement: Social Policy and the Older Worker.* Milton Keynes: Open University Press.

Lankshear, G., Giarchi, G.G. and Cox, S. (2000) *Caring Options for Entering Employment.* University of Plymouth: Community Research Centre.

Lechner, V.M. (1993) 'Support systems and stress reduction among workers caring for dependant parents.' *Social Work 38,* 461–469.

Lewis, J. and Meredith, B. (1988) *Daughters who Care.* London: Routledge.

Lewis, S. (1996) 'Rethinking employment: An organisational culture change framework.' In S. Lewis and J. Lewis (eds) *The Work–Family Challenge: Rethinking Employment.* London: Sage.

Lister, R. (1990) 'Women, economic dependency and citizenship.' *Journal of Social Policy 19,* 4, 445–467.

McLaughlin, E. and Ritchie, J. (1994) 'Legacies of caring: The experiences and circumstances of ex-carers.' *Health and Social Care in the Community 2,* 241–253.

Marks, S. (1994) 'What is a pattern of commitments?' *Journal of Marriage and the Family 56,* 114–115.

Martin, J. and Roberts, C. (1984) *Women and Employment: A Lifetime Perspective.* London: HMSO.

Martire, L.M., Stephens, M.A.P. and Atienza, A.A. (1997) 'The interplay of work and caregiving: Relationship between role satisfaction, role involvement and carergivers' well-being.' *Journal of Gerontology 52b,* 5, 279–289.

Moen, P., Robinson, J. and Dempster-McClain (1995) 'Caregiving and women's well-being: A life course approach.' *Journal of Health and Social Behaviour 36,* 259–273.

Moss, P. (1996) 'Reconciling employment and family responsibilities. A European perspective.' In S. Lewis and J. Lewis (eds) *The Work–Family Challenge: Rethinking Employment.* London: Sage.

Murphy, B., Schofield, H., Nankervis, J., Bloch, S., Herrman, H. and Singh, B. (1997) 'Women with multiple roles: The emotional impact of caring for ageing parents.' *Ageing and Society 17,* 277–291.

Naegele, G. and Reichert, M. (1995) 'Eldercare and the workplace: A new challenge for all social partners in Germany.' In J. Phillips (ed) *Working Carers.* Aldershot: Avebury.

Neal, M.B., Chapman, N.J., Ingersoll-Dayton, B., Emlen, A.C. and Boise, L. (1990) 'Absenteeism and stress among caregivers of the elderly, disabled adults and children.' In D. Biegel and A. Blum (eds) *Aging and Caregiving: Theory, Research and Practice.* Newbury Park CA: Sage.

Nolan, M., Grant, G. and Keady, J. (1997) *Understanding Family Care.* Buckingham: Open University Press.

OPCS (1992) *General Household Survey: Carers in 1990.* Ref. SS 92/2. London: OPCS.

Parker, C. (1993) *With this Body: Caring and Disability in Marriage.* Milton Keynes: Open University Press.

Parker, G. and Lawton, D. (1990) 'Further analysis of the 1985 GHS data on informal care.' SPRU Working Paper 716. York: University of York.

Pearson, M. (1994) *Experience, Skill and Competitiveness: The Implications of an Ageing Population for the Workforce.* Report to the European Foundation for the Improvement of Living and Working Conditions. Dublin: European Foundation for the Improvement of Living and Working Conditions.

Phillips, J. (1993) 'The employment consequences of caring for older people.' *Health and Social Care in the Community 2,* 143–152.

Phillips, J. (ed) (1995) *Working Carers.* Aldershot: Avebury.

Princess Royal Trust for Carers, *The (1995) Carers in Employment.* London: The Carers in Employment Group.

Raabe, P.H. (1996) 'Constructing pluralistic work and career arrangements.' In S. Lewis and J. Lewis (eds) *The Work–Family Challenge: Rethinking Employment.* London: Sage.

Ramsey, D. (1994) 'Carers at Work: A survey of informal care among social work staff at Fife Regional Council.' Unpublished paper.

Russell, P. (1994) 'Access to the system: Support services, financial assistance and practical help for parents of children with disabilities.' In P. Mittler and H. Mittler (eds) *Innovations in Family Support for People with Learning Disabilities.* Chorley: Lisieux Hall Publications.

Scharlach, A. (1994) 'Employment and caregiving: Competing or complementary roles.' *The Gerontologist 34,* 378–385.

Scharlach, A.E., Sobel, E.L. and Roberts, R.E.L. (1991) 'Employment and caregiver strain: An integrative model.' *The Gerontologist 316,* 778–787.

Seddon, D. (1999) 'Negotiating caregiving and employment.' In S. Cox and J. Keady (eds) *Younger People with Dementia: Practice and Development.* London: Jessica Kingsley Publishers.

Shearn, J. (1998) 'Still at home: Participation in paid employment of mothers of children with learning disabilities.' *British Journal of Learning Disabilities 26,* 100–114.

Shearn, J. and Todd, S. (2000) 'Maternal employment and family responsibilities: The perspectives of mothers of children with intellectual disabilities.' *Journal of Applied Research in Intellectual Disabilities 13,* 109–131.

Singleton, J. (2000) 'Women caring for elderly family members. Shaping non-traditional work and family initiatives.' *Journal of Comparative Family Studies 31,* 3, 367–375.

Staines, G.L. (1980) 'Spillover versus compensation: A review of the literature on the relationship between work and non-work.' *Human Relations 33,* 111–129.

Stephens, M.A.P., Franks, M.M. and Atienza, M.M. (1997) 'Where two roles intersect: Spillover between parent care and employment.' *Psychology and Aging 21*, 1, 30–37.

Stephens, M.A.P., Franks, M.M. and Townsend, A.L. (1994) 'Stress and rewards in women's multiple roles: The case of women in the middle.' *Psychology and Aging 9*, 54–62.

Stull, D.E., Kosloski, K., and Kercher, K. (1994) 'Caregiver burden and generic well-being: Opposite sides of the same coin.' *The Gerontologist 34*, 88–94.

Todd, S. and Shearn, J. (1996) 'Struggles with time; the careers of parents of adult sons and daughters with learning disabilities.' *Disability and Society 11*, 379–401.

Warfield, M.E. (2001) 'Employment, parenting and well-being among mothers of children with disabilities.' *Mental Retardation 39*, 4, 207–309.

Whatmore, K. (1989) *Carers at Work.* National Carers Survey. London: Opportunities for Women.

Whittell, B. and Ramcharan, P. (2000) Advocating for Work and Care. Presentation given at Crossroads National Conference. Birmingham, November.

Wright, F.D. (1986) *Left to Care Alone.* Aldershot: Gower.

CHAPTER 8

Getting to Grips with Poor Care

Ann Brechin, Rose Barton and June Stein

Introduction

Care in the community as a policy has raised the profile of unpaid, family caring. There is nothing new in family caring, but naming it as 'care' and making it a focus of government policy shines a spotlight on it. The Carers (Recognition and Services) Act (HMSO 1995) formalised the recognition that carers have rights and needs of their own that do not always coincide with those of the person they seek to support. Those who are seen as 'cared for' are also identified as having their own rights and make a strong case that 'care' is a misleading and indeed harmful concept, implying as it does a dependency and power imbalanced relationship (Morris 1993; Swain and French 1998).

It is difficult territory because of the strong emotions engendered, particularly in the context of families, where there will always be a history of one kind or another feeding into the relationship patterns underlying any care giving or receiving. Social workers, as ever, have to weigh up the needs on both sides. Research evidence is called for to help with such tasks. Evidence is required that addresses how to assess what is needed, how to provide appropriate support for the carers, how to support the individual, how far to try to sustain a fragile relationship, how to judge when the situation is about to break down, and how to read the signals that might indicate abuse and the need to take action to protect someone. Some of this is increasingly forthcoming (see, for example, DoH 1993; Nolan, Grant and Keady 1996; Twigg and Atkin 1994) and much of it is summarised in this book. This chapter, within that broader terrain, takes a family carer perspective on understandings of 'poor' care.

Accounts of care

Popular accounts of care and caring, particularly government policy documents, tend to polarise good care and bad care. It is as if a different lens reveals quite a different picture of what is happening. One lens may reveal the unselfish dedication of carers, showing them as loving and committed, but very stressed and deserving of more support from a relatively neglectful State (HMSO 1995). Another (particularly following revelations of the widespread nature of child abuse) suggests a pattern of 'abuse of vulnerable adults'. This lens reveals that carers cannot be trusted with their vulnerable relatives and the State must ensure greater vigilance to protect people from abuse by relatives, whether physical, psychological, sexual or financial (DoH 1993, 2000). A third lens might be said to show that those seen as 'cared for' in the context of families will have their own way of negotiating the relationship. They may accept the role or feel resentful and oppressed, asserting a primary identity of independent adulthood and rejecting the role and implication of 'burden', a position reflected in the Disability Rights Commission Act (HMSO 1999). To a considerable extent these accounts draw on such different terminology and traditions of thinking as to seem mutually exclusive. Deploying one set of narratives – say the 'dedicated, burdened carer' narrative – makes it hard to hold in mind the parallel reality that some relatives abuse vulnerable members of their family. The alternative narrative – let's call it the 'family abuse' narrative – involves bringing quite a different set of concepts and explanatory frameworks. And, shifting the story again, to the 'care as oppression' narrative, brings quite other frames of reference to bear.

What this does is to put a question mark against the nature of knowledge or evidence in this field of work. Given the increasingly strident calls for evidence-based practice and the undoubted importance of developing and sharing knowledge and understanding, where exactly does this leave us? It is quite hard to know how to make sense of different kinds of evidence drawn from different frames of reference. Yet practitioners out in the field are trying to do this all the time. They are faced with trying to integrate conflicting sets of ideas in order to make sense of what is happening in families and what they ought or ought not to do about it. In the research described below, we were concerned, not so much about evidence of what we know, but more about learning how to think, talk and write about such issues with carers: a kind of 'knowing how' rather than 'knowing that' (see Brechin and Sidell 2000 or Newman and Holzman 1997 for a discussion of these issues).

Looking for the literature

There is a wealth of good research and publications on family care, but finding anything on 'sub-optimal' or 'less than good enough' care proved a challenge. Most of the growing literature about care that is not good enough focuses on abuse, looking at both the incidence and nature of abuse of vulnerable adults by family care givers and attempting to reach some understanding of the factors involved.

Frameworks for multi-agency action designed to ensure that adult abuse is acknowledged and addressed (such as those outlined in 'No Secrets', DoH 2000) provide an important starting point for improving the capacity of service providers to respond appropriately where there are concerns about care. The primary focus, however, is on abuse by paid carers, with family carers mentioned only in passing. The starting point is to assume or promote the disclosure of actual or putative abuse in a way that polarises good care and abuse and makes it difficult to address the uncertain terrain in between. This reflects the fact that workers need to operate with clear guidelines on whether or not particular actions constitute abuse, however difficult these are to apply in practice.

There is evidence to suggest that actual abuse of vulnerable adults is not uncommon (for example, Fulmer *et al.* 1992). Pillemer and Finklehor (1988) investigated the prevalence of elder abuse in the Boston area of the USA, interviewing 2020 elderly people. They found a reported rate of 32 per 1000, with spouses as the most likely perpetrators and roughly equal numbers of men and women as victims. In the first systematic British study, Ogg and Bennett (1992) interviewed 2130 people and found nearly 9 per cent of over 60 year olds reporting recent abuse (verbal, including being shouted at, physical, including general roughness, or financial). They encountered methodological problems including lack of access to the very elderly frail people who are most at risk of abuse. Taking a more focused sample, Wilson (1994), using Brillon's (1987) definitions of abuse, which includes abuse of carers by clients, found 90 abuse referrals out of a caseload of 360 elderly people in an outer London borough.

Consideration of the factors associated with abuse has led to further definitions and formulations, for example, pointing up the interrelationship between macro socio-political factors, ideologies and prejudice and micro-level domestic issues (for example, Penhale and Kingston 1995). Ogg and Munn-Giddings (1993) point out the difficulties, including the methodological and ethical issues, in trying to consider indicators of abuse. The DoH (1993) report does, however, suggest some potential predictive factors:

> Carers under stress, or ill equipped for the caring role, and carers who have been abused themselves, account for a proportion of cases. A history of poor family relationships is a reason for others. (p.17)

Pillemer (1985) suggests that five areas are associated with elder abuse: external stressors, the psychological state of the abuser, social isolation, dependence between the abuser and the abused and transmission of violent behaviours from one generation to another (quoted in Johnson 1996, p.9). Maggs and Laugherne (1996) draw attention to the, often ignored, significance of ageing as a factor in the care of adults with learning disabilities as they and their carers grow older. Increased dependency, both of the cared-for person and the caring relative, are suggested as significant (Pillemer 1985).

Others (Pollock 1994) point to the absence of external support and the degree of 'burden', and Twigg (quoted in Pollock 1994) suggests that the ambiguity of the role adds to the problems and stresses. Coyne, Reichman and Berbig (1993) found, through a questionnaire survey of 342 carers of people with Alzheimer's disease and other dementias, that abuse was associated with high psychological and physical demands. Those abusing were found to have been caring for more years and longer hours and were looking after people who were severely impaired. Although abuse is often assumed to involve some kind of physical harm, Francis (1993) drew on Eastman's model to suggest that emotional abuse is a precursor to, and a form of, actual bodily harm. Blieszner and Schifflet (1990), although not looking at abuse or harm, track the dissolution of relationships following the progression of Alzheimer's disease and suggest that neglect may sometimes ensue.

Research method

The history of the relationship and the transition into caring are often not easy for either party and they may lack money, services and support. Carers are sometimes angry, exhausted or desperate, or perhaps just not well tuned into the feelings and needs of the person they are caring for. Love, commitment and appreciation are often intermingled with anger, frustration and despair. As one carer, who took part in one of our discussion groups, observed, 'I mean a nurse trains, a social worker trains, but we people – normal people, ordinary people – don't train for this, so we don't really know how to react to that kind of situation.'

To talk in terms of abuse is not likely to be well received by carers, even if the experience on the receiving end may well feel quite abusive and the consequences may be quite damaging and painful – often for both parties. Our research set out to engage in discussion of suboptimal care with carers. This set us a methodological challenge in seeking to engage directly in discussion of such sensitive matters. The danger was that any mention of abuse might result in a splitting off into the good care versus abusive care polarities with a resistance then to engage with ideas about or experiences of suboptimal care.

We found ourselves stuck for words at the outset, particularly words that would be acceptable to use in talking with carers. There are many shades and qualities of care within the complexity of family life and many care relationships might be seen as suboptimal and even abusive at times, without attracting an 'abuse' label. Our impetus was to focus on the 'grey' area in the middle. Defining it by what it was not, we could say it was not about 'good' or even fairly good care and it was not about seriously bad care or 'abuse', as it would normally be defined. We could not just borrow from the 'dedicated, burdened carer' narrative and stretch it to include situations where the burden was too great and care began to break down or become unsustainable. We did not exclude such situations and we did find ourselves in that territory a lot of the time. We explicitly, however, wanted to move beyond that relative comfort zone into describing and discussing care relationships where the interactions were not easily justifiable by being put down to stress. An initial and significant challenge was simply to find any acceptable terms at all to describe our interest and focus. How should we or could we talk to family carers about this? What words were available that would be close enough to what was intended without giving offence?

We looked, naturally, to the research literature to help us. This preamble reflects a lengthy process of initial exploration including a feasibility study (Chamberlain 1998) revealing the depth of the difficulties that language and the associated polarisations presented to us. It was a significant first hurdle. If we expected to get people talking to us about such issues we had to begin to find the right words, or at least some words, ourselves to get started. Because of our struggle to stay outside the available frames of reference (or dominant narratives) for discussing care, we found ourselves more and more aware of the extent to which research was embedded in such frames. That is not to imply it was narrow or irrelevant – far from it, as the literature review has indicated. But the effect was to lead us frequently to the conclusion that it could not offer us the answers we were looking for.

We arrived eventually at a number of phrases that seemed to work and helped us to engage in discussions with carers, with care support workers and social workers and with other interested researchers. The phrases we used most often in explaining the research to carers, when negotiating access, for example, were that we wanted to find out more about '*difficulties in care relationships*' or about times '*when things go wrong*'. We also latterly found ourselves using the description '*care that might give cause for concern*', and, more for ourselves as a useful shorthand, '*suboptimal care*'. This could be seen, though such phrases are not at all precise, as sitting close to, but across the line from, 'good enough care'. We were conscious of the risk of using euphemisms for abuse, but this, in essence, is about care that probably is not good enough.

A second challenge for us was to consider the ethical issues involved in probing such relationships. How far is it justifiable for us or for support workers to intervene in adult family relationships? What standards apply when relatives care for someone at home? To acknowledge deficits in the care being given may mean implicitly criticising the carer. And even if concerns can be addressed openly workers may not have the skills or resources to help. And yet to fail to acknowledge the extent to which suboptimal care may be experienced as harmful or abusive – even when hurt is not intended – is to fail to recognise the rights and needs of those who are dependent on others' care.

The research study that underpins this chapter faced a challenge that went right to the heart of the issue – how to talk about potentially damaging aspects of caring without making carers guilty, fearful or defensive. Admitting to difficulties in caring is not easy. The media often portrays carers as totally dedicated and selfless, and talking openly about shortcomings shatters this myth. Carers also fear that disclosures to health and social care workers may lead to unwelcome interventions rather than help, and they may find reassurances about the confidentiality of research difficult to accept.

We carried out research interviews in four locations: Bedfordshire, Hertfordshire, Kent and Norfolk. Carers were contacted through social services and private and voluntary organisations in each area. Individual interviews and group discussions were based on six vignettes or 'mini-stories' depicting care scenarios. These were developed from anonymised real-life situations adapted to reflect a range of 'difficult moments'. These vignettes (see below) were designed to be open to different interpretations and were intended to generate discussion about how carers make sense of suboptimal care.

Box 8.1 Vignette 1: The pyjama trousers

A looks after her husband, B, who has become very confused and forgetful. B goes to a day centre where he seems quite settled, but getting him up and dressed in time for the transport is very difficult. He is not able to dress himself but is also very resistant to being helped. He particularly dislikes removing his pyjama trousers and very often ends up with his trousers on top of his pyjamas as the only solution. Once, he had kept the same pyjamas on for two weeks and eventually his wife 'accidentally on purpose' spilled a glass of water over him from behind. It had the desired effect in that he wanted to change at once, but he was extremely angry, seemed convinced that she had done it on purpose (which she had, of course) and they both became very upset.

Box 8.2 Vignette 2: A drink in the night

D is in his late 30s, still lives at home, and attends a day centre for adults with learning disabilities. He copes with many aspects of his life, but continues to have a tendency to be incontinent at night. He seemed to have been doing better until his parents realised that he was getting out of bed and weeing in a corner of his bedroom. After that, his father tried to wake if he heard D moving and was usually in time to make sure he went through to the toilet. On one occasion he was too late but managed to control his frustration as he led his son through to the toilet, changed him and then went through to mop up. When he came back D had poured himself a glass of water. His father told him very firmly that the last thing he needed was to drink more water, took the glass from him and poured it down the sink.

Box 8.3 Vignette 3: The tape recorder

G is a young woman in her late twenties with a learning disability. Her mother gave up work to look after her, as no suitable day services were available when she left school. Both mother and daughter are bored and lonely, and their relationship has become strained because her mother finds G's speech hard to understand. One afternoon G made several attempts to tell her mother something, but her mother couldn't work it out and kept asking G to repeat it. G got more and more angry and started shouting 'stupid' at the top of her voice. Her mother felt she was being blamed unfairly and put a cassette into her tape player to record G's speech. When she played the tape back G was horrified at how slurred her speech sounded and burst into tears.

Box 8.4 Vignette 4: Cooking with hot oil

J was in the kitchen cooking supper with her mother, K, who is elderly with mild dementia, sitting at the table watching her. J tries very hard to keep K out of the way when she is cooking but K loves to be near her. In fact K cannot bear to let her daughter out of her sight. Just as J was about to tip the potatoes into a pan of hot oil, K came up behind her and started trying to give her a hug. As J pushed her out of the way K lost her balance and fell, hitting her head on the corner of the table and bruising her eye. Although K quickly settled down and didn't seem upset about what had happened, her daughter was worried about what other people would think.

Box 8.5 Vignette 5: The chair

L looks after his elderly wife M who has mental health problems. L keeps all the drink locked away in a cupboard upstairs but M keeps wandering around the house and upsetting things looking for drink and believing she is in prison. When L was in the bathroom one day, M broke the glass door of the sideboard and had to go to hospital for stitches. Ever since, L ties M into a chair whenever he goes upstairs for more than a few minutes and is unable to persuade her to go with him. Although M is very distressed when her movement is restricted, L feels it is necessary for M's safety.

Box 8.6 Vignette 6: The spoon and fork

Z has a learning disability and lives with her parents and two younger brothers. She left school last year where she made enormous progress and learnt more skills than her parents ever thought possible. Z is a messy eater and always, when she gets the chance, eats with her hands instead of a spoon and fork. Her parents would prefer her to use cutlery but try to be patient with her. One evening, when the family were eating a meal together, Z's father got so exasperated that he slammed the spoon and fork down in front of her and put his head in his hands. Z picked up the fork and jabbed her father's arm, causing it to bleed. He raised his hand to hit her, but managed to control himself. Z burst into tears.

There were 12 focus groups involving 82 participants. Forty carers were also interviewed individually. The carers ranged in age from 41 to 84, with the younger carers being the parents or children of the person they cared for and the older carers usually caring for a spouse or partner. Of those cared for, 18 elderly people had dementia and 4 had other illnesses, 14 younger people had learning disabilities of some form and 1 young person had mental health problems. The carers were 26 women and 14 men. Of the 21 women being cared for, 8 had a female as their main carer, 2 had the caring shared by a female and a male, and 9 are cared for by a male. One man cared for both his daughter and his wife. Of the 16 men, 14 are cared for by a female carer and 2 are cared for by both a male and a female.

Research findings

This method of using vignettes offered a way of generating discussion about a range of 'difficult' care situations as well as eliciting personal narratives. At the individual interviews as well as the group meetings, carers were asked to rank the vignettes according to the level of concern raised by the situation described. Although the rankings of vignettes showed surprisingly little consistency, asking carers to account for their ranking of the vignettes revealed many shared discourses.

What was interesting was the extent to which interpretations and responses were formulated through discussion and reflection. Initial reactions evolved into more considered and sophisticated debate in which seeing both sides was valued as important. This might mean an initial shocked expression of disapproval, 'I think that's absolutely terrible' or 'I would never dream of doing such a thing' (tying someone in a chair), to later reflections on how sometimes imposing restrictions for somebody's safety can be necessary or a discussion of concern about the timescale, or the availability of other options, or the issue of isolation.

Initial analysis indicated a number of themes that emerged consistently. The most frequently mentioned were those relating to factors contributing to carer stress. Exhaustion, frustration and the relentlessness of the demands on time and energy were mentioned over and over again combined with a recognition of the importance of emotional and practical support. Experience of this varied widely, with some expressions of great appreciation of support received alongside others who felt their needs were unrecognised.

Alongside this unsurprising emphasis on themes of burden and stress as signifiers of concern were a number of other themes. What emerged was a multifaceted discussion of 'poor' care and of when and why it should give cause for concern. No single person articulated the whole of such a picture, but within discussions these were the themes that emerged with surprising regularity and consistency.

1. *Stress themes* raising issues of frustration, exhaustion and the relentlessness of demands over long periods of time:

> It was such a little thing really…she just was being a bit messy (the fork story) but we've all been there.

> When you're just at the end of your tether.

> I would be very concerned about that…because it's an ongoing situation.

2. *Rights themes* including concern about lack of respect, or unjustified restrictions to the freedom of the individual being cared for:

> What would be the effect on the other person that it is happening to because that is the crux of it isn't it? And it is sort of taking away his rights isn't it?

> You wouldn't like it yourself.

The absence of 'respect' was another frequently raised reason for concern, often leading to a higher than expected ranking for the 'glass of water' story

3. *Risk or outcome themes,* including strategies for reducing risk:

A frequent refrain in relation to the 'cooking with hot oil' story was:

> You just don't cook chips.

Another frequent comment in relation to 'the chair' story was:

> Don't have drink in the house.

Failure to ensure a measure of protection to attend to basic environmental safety was seen also as a matter of concern:

> I had to keep the doors locked. My husband would have escaped and I couldn't leave him even if I wanted to post a letter.

But it was not seen as unproblematic:

> I don't think it is a good thing to restrict them because they get so frustrated.

4. *Relationship-focused themes* which saw the underlying quality of the relationship as the most significant indicator – an indication that a relationship might be breaking down or that communication was a serious problem – caused a lot of concern and often led to a ranking of emotional risk (for example, the 'tape recorder' story) much higher than physical risk (for example, the 'hot oil' story). There was also a clear recognition of the importance of the prior relationship:

> So all I'm saying is, what I'm really saying is, I suppose, that we all drag along a lot of history. And the history that we drag along, and I suppose the older you get, the more history you've got dragging along, and the more, you know, it's all influencing your attitudes and the way you behave towards them.

> If you love them it's not a problem.

> It sounds almost cruel, but, you know, I just…I can't feel the same way about her that some people might have done who have had a really good relationship because then you'd just be feeling so sad that you've lost the person she used to be.

5. *Morality themes* about blame, guilt and responsibility:

> It's no good being angry.

> You just have to deal with it.

> You have to keep your focus on the person.

This led to concern about what was seen as unreasonable expectation or blame (for example, 'the fork' and 'the tape recorder'). It also, however, led to concern about balance in how carers view themselves:

> I have been most disgusted with myself at times, I think I am getting a wee bit better, but sometimes there is something, a sort of flash point.

> Yes, but even so in a sense we are entitled to have feelings, and if they are not always under control, well it is part of our humanity.

> You have to be forgiving of yourself.

> It isn't easy.

The ambiguity of the vignettes enabled a whole range of interpretations to come into view. Instead of jumping to conclusions by blaming the carer or leaping to the carer's defence, these stories encouraged more complex and thoughtful analyses to emerge. Complex and nuanced accounts were negotiated in focus groups or elaborated by individuals as they reflected aloud, drawing on these discourses and yielding rich transcripts in which the construction of meanings of 'poor' care were illuminated.

Co-constructing an ethics of care

Dominant or fixed understandings of care – about good or abusive care, for example – can be understood as occurring within a context of ethical beliefs which determine a sense of what ought to be happening. On that basis one could derive a sense of the logic that drives the story, particularly in terms of rights or wrongs. It may be seen as wrong to tie someone into her chair and exploring why might suggest the pre-existence of ideas about human rights, justice and freedom of movement. Where such positions become fixed, this leads to rigid ideas about what ought and ought not to be done – sometimes referred to as 'hardening of the oughteries'!

Another way of looking at this, however, is to see the development of the account as part of a process of constructing the logic and the ethics. This involves a shift from seeing the ethics *as* context to seeing the ethics being constructed *in* context. Conversations and dialogue (whether casual or part of research interviews or focus groups) allow interpretations and accounts to emerge through a form of joint action. This is what seemed to occur in the process of our interviews and focus groups: what social constructionists writing in Shotter and Gergen's edited collection (1989) or in the more therapeutically focused collection by McNamee and Gergen (1992), would describe as 'performing ethics'. In this analysis, interactions between people are the place to look to see where ethical work and thinking is created. Perhaps what happened here was a process of dialogue that supported carers in opening up and challenging fixed accounts.

Our interviews with carers also touched on the circumstances in which they felt that compulsory professional intervention in private family relationships was justifiable. The carers we spoke to had diverse views but emphasised that those professionally involved need to build up good relationships with the families they work with. They valued workers who really understood the carer's situation, were aware of the history and complexity of the caring relationship and could be relied upon to listen to the carer's point of view. There also needed to be understanding and respect for other people's way of life – respect for their beliefs, fears and aspirations as well as their language, culture and religion. This could be read as a recognition of the value of professional workers and carers 'performing ethics', that is, constructing an ethics of care together, unique to a particular situation.

A serious consideration here is the extent to which the voice of the person being cared for can remain core to the process. If ethical positions are not taken as fixed there is always a concomitant, perceived danger of 'going soft on abuse'. In this study the focus has been on the carers. Others (Forbat 2002) have embarked on the challenging task of exploring difficulties in care relationships with both carers and those being cared for, listening to how each partner in the dyad constructs the relationship and the nature of the caring.

A striking aspect of this study was the fact that carers responded so positively to the chance to talk openly with other carers and with us. Listening to other people's accounts of 'not coping very well' helped carers to validate their own struggles and alleviate self-blame. The tears that punctuated meetings were not always triggered by sadness. The sheer awfulness of some of the scenarios recounted meant that some people laughed until they cried – or sometimes cried until they laughed. Many of the carers spoke in very moving terms of the history of the relationship, their strong bond and sense of enduring commitment; others spoke of longstanding difficulties. As they left the meetings, carers frequently described 'walking on air', and feelings of 'relief' and 'elation'. And all this stemmed from a relatively short period of time spent in a setting where it was possible to talk openly about all aspects of the caring role, including intimate, personal details.

Gathering information and building evidence in relation to sensitive human experiences will always be unpredictable and carry risks. Allowing ethical frameworks to evolve rather than assuming them to be pre-determined seemed to be a key factor in opening the door to discussing poor care with carers. Government policy is already advocating dedicated and burdened carers on the one hand (DoH 1995) and recognising and tackling abuse on the other (DoH 2000). This research suggests a way of engaging with the sensitive and complex territory that lies between.

References

Blieszner, R. and Schifflet, P.A. (1990) 'The effects of Alzheimer's Disease on close relationships between patients and caregivers.' *Family Relations 39*, 1, 57–63.

Brechin, A. and Sidell, M. (2000) 'Ways of knowing.' In R. Gomm and C. Davies *Using Evidence in Health and Social Care*. London: Sage.

Brillon, Y. (1987) *Victimization and Fear of Crime among the Elderly*. Toronto: Butterworths.

Chamberlain, A. (1998) 'The Breakdown of Care in the Home – a pre-pilot study.' Unpublished report, Milton Keynes: School of Health and Social Welfare, The Open University.

Coyne, A.C., Reichman, W. and Berbig, L. (1993) 'The relationship between dementia and elder abuse.' *American Journal of Psychiatry 150*, 4, Apr 93, 643–646.

DoH (Department of Health) (1993) *No Longer Afraid: The Safeguarding of Older People in Domestic Settings*. London: The Stationery Office.

DoH (Department of Health) (1995) *Carers (Recognition and Services) Act 1995: Policy Guidance/Practice Guide*. London: The Stationery Office.

DoH (Department of Health) (2000) *No Secrets: Guidance on Developing and Implementing Multi-agency Policies and Procedures to Protect Vulnerable Adults from Abuse*. London: Department of Health.

Forbat, E. (2002) Exploring Accounts of Care: Two Sides of the Story. Unpublished PhD Thesis, The Open University.

Francis, J.(1993) 'Where do you draw the line?' *Community Care (967)* 20 May, 18–19.

Fulmer, T.T., McMahon, D.J., Baer-Hines, M. and Forget, B. (1992) 'Abuse, neglect, abandonment, violence and exploitation: An analysis of all elderly patients seen in one emergency department during a six-month period.' *Journal of Emergency Nursing 18*, 505–510.

HMSO (1995) Carers (Recognition and Services) Act.

HMSO (1999) Disability Rights Commission Act.

Johnson, J.R. (1996) 'Risk factors associated with negative interactions between family caregivers and elderly care-receivers.' *International Journal of Ageing and Human Development 43*, 1, 7–20.

McNamee, S. and Gergen, K. (eds) (1992) *Therapy as Social Construction*. London: Sage.

Maggs C. and Laugharne C. (1996) 'Relationship between elderly carers and the older adult with learning disabilities: An overview of the literature.' *Journal of Advanced Nursing 23*, 2, February, 243–251.

Morris, J. (1993) *Community Care or Independent Living?* York: Joseph Rowntree Foundation.

Newman, F. and Holzman, L. (1997) *The End of Knowing – A New Developmental Way of Learning*. London: Routledge.

Nolan, M., Grant, G. and Keady, J. (1996) *Understanding Family Care: A Multidimensional Model of Caring and Coping*. Buckingham: Open University Press.

Ogg, J. and Bennett, G. (1992) 'Elder abuse in Britain.' *BMJ (305)*, October, 998–999.

Ogg, J. and Munn-Giddings, C. (1993) 'Researching elder abuse.' *Ageing and Society 13*, 3, 389–413.

Penhale, B. and Kingston, P. (1995) 'Social perspectives on elder abuse.' In P. Kingston and B. Penhale (eds) *Family, Violence and the Caring Professions*. London: Macmillan.

Pillemer, K. (1985) 'The dangers of dependency: New findings on domestic violence against the elderly.' *Social Problems 33*, 2, December 1985.

Pillemer, K. and Finkelhor, D. (1988) 'The prevalence of elder abuse: A random sample survey.' *Gerontologist 28*, (February), 51.

Pollock A. (1994) 'Carers' literature review.' *Nursing Times 90*, 25, 22 June, 31–33.

Shotter, J. and Gergen, K. (1989) (eds) *Texts of Identity*. London: Sage.

Swain, J. and French, S. (1998) 'Normality and disabling care.' In A. Brechin, J. Wlamsley, J. Katz and S. Peace (eds) *Care Matters, Concepts, Practice and Research in Health and Social Care*. London: Sage.

Twigg, J. and Atkin, K. (1994) *Carers Perceived: Policy and Practice in Informal Care*. Buckingham: Open University Press.

Wilson, G. (1994) 'Abuse of elderly men and women among clients of a community psychogeriatric service.' *British Journal of Social Work 24*, 6, 681–700.

CHAPTER 9

The Legal Framework of Caring

Margaret Ross

Introduction

Law and ethics form an interwoven backdrop to all aspects of caring. Applied imaginatively and flexibly they provide empowerment within the caring process, but equally can form a straightjacket if applied rigidly and dogmatically. They have been the subject of extensive development in recent years: in law to reflect reforms in political and social approaches to caring and, in ethics, to mould traditional ethical frameworks to home-based rather than hospital-based care.

At the same time as the law has been undergoing reform to enable and regulate organisational change in health and social care, there has been extensive empirical research into the experiences and wishes of those for whom care is required (increasingly termed 'users' of services within the public social care setting, although that term is not applied routinely in the legal or ethical context). Professionals who are responsible for planning and/or delivering that care and individuals who provide it in whole or in part are also drawn into evaluative processes. Indeed Stalker *et al.* (1999), in a research study reviewing the views of users and carers about services for people with learning difficulties, noted some 'evaluation fatigue' not least on the part of carers in contrast to the desire for greater involvement in decisions concerning the service users. Little of the research has had *as its focus* the law or ethics as they operate for users and the caring relationship. Substantial reviews of legislation and safeguards in the fields of mental health and incapacity have focused attention on a number of vital issues of law and practice for users and carers. Carers have consistently featured in the body of persons whose views have been canvassed about legislation, their focus being involvement, information and access to services. The acknowledgement of carer views is rarely coupled with any frank examination of the conflicts between carer imperatives and user imperative. Hence, in recent reviews of legislation, user-centred principles of autonomy, minimum intervention and confidentiality sit unhappily with principles of respect for carers. There is very little attention paid to the situations in which these principles will conflict and the mechanisms that might be applied to deal with those conflicts in reality.

However, there appears to be some hesitation over articulating and addressing the breadth of legal and ethical challenges that carers may face, and indeed should embrace for the benefit of the user. Concern was articulated by Kapp (1991) who notes the non-existence of 'useful literature' then addressing the range of legal ramifications of family care giving in the United States. It is still hard to find any single source of legal and ethical analysis focussing on the tensions between user priorities, service providers and the carer's role. McKay and Patrick (1995) and Griffiths and Roberts (1995) use the growth in community care as a context within which to flag up, amongst other things, the rights and duties of persons cared for due to disability or age and their carers. Wells and Freer (1988), Eekelaar and Pearl (1989) and Arber and Evandrou (1993) examine some challenges for social policy and law arising from an ageing population. McHale (1998) offers comments on confidentiality for the purposes of review of the Mental Health Act 1983. Stalker *et al.* (1999) noted that some carers wished to be informed about decisions concerning their disabled children who were now in adulthood and were entitled to respect for autonomy, and recent studies regarding direct payments for services show that carers' motives for wishing direct payment may be very different from the motives of users. Many studies offer useful insights but there is not a coming together of material on the range of legal and ethical challenges that may arise in all caring situations.

The end of the twentieth century saw a spurt of activity in relation to the updating and regulating of statutes around private caring arrangements, informed by data from pre-legislative reviews and consultations. These go some way to address concerns raised by Kapp (1991), but in other respects bring the issues into sharper focus. Much concerning the actual legal and ethical decision-making process between user and carer appears still to be left to assumption. Research on the extent and quality of delivery of service for carers and users is in something of a vacuum if it is not complemented by frank examination of how the law and ethics operate to facilitate or inhibit decisions affecting care.

The caring arena – development of legal interventions

The legislative focus on carers has arisen following the increase in reliance on care provision in the home or community. Whilst the words 'care in the community' are linked, often pejoratively, to the introduction of Community Care Orders in the mental health sphere, government initiatives for private care and carers have proliferated since 1990.[1] The community care order philosophy was for multidisciplinary planning of care to include those involved as informal or unpaid carers who are to play a substantial part in the care of the individual in the community.[2] The extent of use of community care in a variety of contexts has been the subject of research (Bowes and Dar 2000; MacDonald 1999; Millan 2001; Petch *et al.* 1996; Richardson 1999).

Prior to legislative acknowledgments of the carer's role, in the context of contributing to a state-monitored care plan, caring for other adults was essentially a matter of private ordering or family duty. Caring for children was more regulated by statute from the early part of the twentieth century due to an overt recognition that the vulnerability of a child due to youth would warrant statutory interference in the caring process, but the same could not be said of private care for vulnerable adults. Dependency upon a carer of a person in need of care may have been less readily assumed then than it is now: often the carer had much to gain in security of accommodation and board, loss of which was sometimes compensated by legacy when the person under their care died. Except in the event of dispute over property, it would not be expected that information about private care arrangements, and their strengths or tensions, would be in the public domain.

As the public law surrounding carers has developed it has tried to embrace this heritage of privacy and individual choice. This presents challenges for decision making in reality, since the process of care planning, supported by public services and commercial care agencies, extends so widely beyond the user and individual carers. There is an implicit need on the part of health and social work agencies to keep individual carers 'on board'. Delivering a care service to the liking of the user or within available resources might be difficult without the carer's contribution. This may have inhibited individuals and professionals from raising and addressing the potential legal and ethical tensions between the carer and the user. There appears also to be a lack of baseline understanding of the legal and ethical framework not only on the part of individuals but also professionals (Atkinson and Patterson 2000; Churchill *et al.* 1999; Gilmore *et al.* 1994; Millan 2001; Wall *et al.* 1999), yet such understanding is essential for meaningful planning and delivery of care by both professionals and individuals. This also makes it difficult to design and implement research studies.

In their research review carried out for the Expert Committee on the Review of the Mental Health Act, Churchill *et al.* (1999) noted that there was little research in relation to evaluating the impact of most legislative provisions. In the context of examination of Part III of the Mental Health Act 1983, the researchers comment that

> [Q]uantitative methodology alone will never be able to answer questions regarding the appropriateness of present legislation. There is a need for a combination of qualitative and quantitative approaches to examine the use of the Act by professionals and the experience of patients before any overall conclusions regarding the appropriateness of present legislation can be drawn.

It is suggested that this comment is equally relevant to a broader range of caring situations but that critical evaluation of the carer's role and experience is vital to that process. Extensive review has been carried out in recent years in the context of mental health (Millan 2001; Richardson 1999), learning disability (Scottish Executive 2000), incapacity (Law Commission of England and Wales 1995; Scottish Law Commission 1995) and personal care for older people (Leontaridi 2002; Stearns and Butterworth 2002; Sutherland Committee 1999). It has been recognised that the legislative frameworks or common law rules governing many adults who require care are out of line with modern models of delivery of care. The carer's role is now acknowledged in various pieces of legislation and a fairly consistent definition of legislatively recognised 'carer' has emerged.

Who is a carer?

An individual who provides or intends to provide a substantial amount of care on a regular basis for another person meets the statutory definition of carer as provided in the first piece of legislation dedicated to the legal rights of carers – The Carers (Recognition and Services) Act 1995.[3] This Act applies throughout Great Britain. The Carers and Disabled Children Act 2000 uses the same definition, but it extends only to England and Wales. The same definition is found in the Community Care and Health (Scotland) Act passed by the Scottish Parliament in February 2002 and, in paraphrase, in the Regulation of Care (Scotland) Act 2001. In each case it excludes those individuals who provide care by virtue of a contract of employment or other contract with any person or, as a volunteer for a voluntary organisation.[4] In Scotland the term 'primary carer' identifies a person (or organisation) who may receive information about an adult with incapacity and it is proposed that the term be carried forward into new mental health legislation. This may to some extent relieve the possible tension when two or more carers claim that each of them provides a substantial amount of care on a regular basis. However it has been noted that the general definition of carer (including primary carer) may not reflect the sporadic (although at times intense) role for carers of those with a mental illness (Millan 2001). The definition is clearly focused upon the carer with no regard for 'another person' for whom care is provided.

The words on which the definition of carer depends are to be interpreted in their everyday sense and as a matter of fact rather than law – hence there is no minimum specification of what amounts to 'substantial' or 'regular' and these may vary according to the nature and level of care that is needed by a particular person. Many other pieces of legislation dedicated to the regulation of care refer to the 'carer' or to the dependency of one person on the care of another[5] but in the main they too rely upon a factual assessment of care.[6] The exception is benefits legislation, where a minimum amount of caring time is specified in order to trigger certain exemptions or benefits.[7]

As the legislation concerning carers becomes integral to the legislative web of health and social care, it is encouraging to note the consistency of definition but with the flexibility to encompass the widest possible range of individual caring arrangements. However, policy makers need to be continually informed about the nature and extent of private caring roles. Focus in older legislation upon nearest relatives, or next of kin, for certain important decision making, displacing the carer with the legally recognised nearest person, is gradually giving way to more broadly defined relationships involving, for example, a homosexual partner (Millan 2001), and options for an individual to nominate those who will participate in care giving and decision making in the event of the individual's incapacity (Law Commission 1995; Scottish Law Commission 1995).

Needs of carers

In addition to providing for involvement of carers in the planning and delivery of care, the law has been developed to reflect the resultant needs of carers, hence needs assessment for carers became a statutory right,[8] limited at first to cases in which a community care assessment for the user is being undertaken and the carer has specifically requested the assessment. The right to assessment of needs carries no right to the needs of the carer being met, but they must be taken into account in planning for the person to be cared for. Millan (2001) noted that most carers in Scotland had not been assessed, principally due to lack of awareness of the right, but that the Strategy for Carers in Scotland contained a commitment on the part of the Scottish Executive to enable carers to have needs assessed directly (independent of the assessment of needs of the cared for person). While the issue of information is addressed in the Community Care and Health (Scotland) Act by introducing a statutory duty upon health authorities to have and disseminate a carers' information strategy, other provisions in the act concerning needs assessment for carers are still driven by the ability or inability of that carer to deliver the care needed. There is to be a right of the carer to be assessed for need without there being in place a process of assessment of user need, but the question of how the carer's need is to be met is to be considered *vis-à-vis* planning for the user, so the truly independent needs assessment for the carer remains somewhat elusive. The requirement to seek an assessment is in itself a potential source of conflict for the altruistic carer who may be inhibited from making the request by focusing upon the needs, and wishes of the user. Evidence shows that carers do suppress tensions between their caring role and, for example, employment opportunities or other ambitions (Leontaridi 2002).

Strategic initiatives for carers have emerged; 1999 saw the publication of a National Strategy for Carers for England and Wales (Department of Health 1999) and the Scottish Executive's Strategy for Carers (Scottish Executive 1999). These were followed in Scotland by a pre-legislative consultation process focusing upon carers and in England by publication of a Charter for Long Term Care aimed at users and carers (DoH 2000). Government-initiated information services and alliances of interested agencies go some way to empower carers through networking; reviews involving carers highlighted the fact that information about rights to services often arose from other carers rather than service providers or agencies (Scottish Executive 2000; Stalker et al. 1999). Networking of agencies concerned with the interests of users and carers was used to direct legislative effect in the form of the Adults with Incapacity (Scotland) Act 2000. Although Law Commissions on both sides of the border reported to similar effect in 1995, recommending a simplified but regulated process for administering the affairs and welfare decisions of incapacitated adults, both reports were set aside. The creation of a Scottish Parliament in 1999 with devolved powers on health issues provided the scope for parliamentary attention (and indeed health and social care issues have remained at the forefront of that parliament's work ever since).

The Adults with Incapacity (Scotland) Act 2000 is novel in taking a principled approach to addressing the needs of adults, an approach that is now quite well established in childcare law. This approach is proposed for renewed mental health legislation in England and in Scotland. It goes some way towards flushing out the legal and ethical issues that arise in the context of caring for adults but, it is argued, provides no new mechanisms for dealing with the tensions to which they give rise.

A principled approach

Kapp (1991) identifies belief in reciprocity and the principle of beneficence as potentially conflicting ethical norms in the caring situation. He warns of the dangers of a 'power of dependency' caused by the compassion level that will exist, or be expected, on the part of a family care giver as opposed to a professional care giver. Kapp's message is to confront and manage, rather than ignore, the potential for dependency or conflict. Morris (1993) notes that family care giving is potentially destructive of the autonomy of both care giver and user. In the legislative approaches that are finding acceptance in the United Kingdom, the ethical norms of reciprocity and beneficence are set alongside minimum intervention, autonomy, consultation (including with carers) and reasonableness of intended action (Law Commission 1995; Scottish Law Commission 1995). In England the proposed principles are coupled with a general test of best interest of the user, akin to the best interest test that is familiar in child law. However for decisions concerning an adult, that best interest test should not be paramount (Millan 2001). It is recognised that whilst a third party should not be making decisions that are not in the best interest (viewed objectively) of the user, the user may, and often will, exercise autonomy within the bounds of his or her capacity to make a decision that, arguably, is not in his or her best interest, for example, to smoke or drink to the danger of health.

Mental health reforms in Scotland (Millan 2001) contain proposals for a lengthier list of principles although in similar vein but, dealing as they must with compulsory intervention in care, they include justice-based principles of non-discrimination, equality, respect for diversity and reciprocity and autonomy-based principles of informality as against compulsion, participation, but also respect for carers (to include information and advice for the carer, but also to have regard to the carer's views and needs). The reforms also call for principles based on beneficence and non-malificence in the form of least restrictive intervention coupled with benefit not reasonably achievable under a less restrictive intervention (Millan 2001). It is recognised that these principles will at times be in conflict with each other, but it is intended that they be applied horizontally rather than vertically with no one principle being presumptively more influential than the other. It is anticipated that, for example, application of one principle might assist in deciding a conflict between others (Scottish Executive 2001). These principles will have to be interpreted in accordance with principles of Human Rights legislation, through which the core values of the European Convention on Human Rights ('convention rights') are incorporated into law enforceable against public authorities in the United Kingdom.[9] Thus, privacy and family life are protected, and intrusions upon them must be fully explained and justified. Procedures by which a final decision is made affecting convention rights must be fair, and parties whose rights are to be affected by the decision must have equality of access to the information used in the process. While clearly this entitles the user to the fullest information about decision making, access to information by the carer would have to be justified (McHale 1998) in accordance with rights of the carer, for example to occupy the home of the user.

Principles and carer involvement

Clearly it is desirable that carers receive information and advice with the purpose of delivering best available care for the user, and it appears that this process is underway, although its effectiveness will have to be monitored and evaluated. More difficult is the issue of the carer's views and needs which inevitably will conflict with those of the user at times, and how that issue can and will be addressed in the overall balancing of principles. When considering a right for primary carers to receive information about the service user for whom they care, Millan (2001) noted that the breach of patient confidentiality which this would entail would be justified in certain circumstances on the basis that it would be needed to fulfil the caring role in general (not merely in order to prevent risk or assure safety which is the established excuse for breach of confidentiality). The concern about this is by no means confined to influences upon legislative change (Kapp 1991; Murphy 1998). In research undertaken to obtain views on delivery of funding for personal care in Scotland, the views of users were focused upon reliable and available care, offered in a manner acceptable to the user (MacDonald 1999), whether or not by direct payment. In contrast, many carers valued the concept of direct payment to carers (now provided for in the Community Care and Health (Scotland) Act) in order that they might have the liberty to organise and pay for substitute care to meet their own needs for a break from normal caring tasks (Stearns and Butterworth 2002). To assume naively, as the law appears to do, that such a difference would not arise, is the fundamental mistake, and research studies designed to uncover the real motivations of those involved in the caring process (individual and professional) are to be welcomed.

Modern legislation in Scotland draws only fine distinctions between private carers and the provision of care by service providers, whether public bodies such as social work departments, the NHS or voluntary or commercial agencies. The Commission for the Regulation of Care, brought into operation on 1 April 2002, has a responsibility to monitor care however it is provided, and its range is so broad that it is engaging in discussion with the many other agencies with overlapping functions. However, it is novel in the care of adults to have a regulatory process for care provided privately, by friends or family care givers. The equivalent English legislation is limited to public sector and commercial providers of care. In the Scottish Adults with Incapacity regime, all powers of attorney granted by adults before incapacity must be registered with the Public Guardian in Scotland before they can be acted upon, and powers of attorney dealing with personal welfare issues must also be intimated to the Mental Welfare Commission. It has a duty to provide advice when requested and to monitor the operation of the power of attorney particularly if concern is expressed over the personal welfare of the adult. This again brings private ordering of care planning for adults into the public regulatory arena. Anecdotal evidence from legal professionals in private practice to date suggests that individuals who might have participated in care management as private attorneys in the past, are put off by the perception of bureaucratic accountability, which may lead to greater use of welfare guardianship involving the public sector.

Kapp (1991) counsels against attempting to draw personal carers namely, family care givers, into the regulatory mechanisms, unless there are substantial data to justify the cost and disruption that this would entail. It might be argued that this is an inevitable consequence of recognising the rights and obligations of carers and of their active participation in a package of care. However, there are many conflicting messages. Terminology that one associates with the nuclear family – of conscience, moral obligation, protection, responsibilities and rights to fulfil those responsibilities – may be lost in the administratively driven processes of care planning. This appears to be more evident in processes of making decisions involving the carer and responsible agencies, but can be resisted while networking with other carers (Scottish Executive 2000), where traditional norms can be reinforced and strength obtained with which to handle the 'care maze' (McKay and Patrick 1995). Compulsory detentions from home under mental health legislation have been found to occur very often as a result of carer inability to cope (Churchill *et al.* 1999; Gilmore *et al.* 1994). Legislation currently provides for nearest relatives (who may or may not include the primary carer) to consent to emergency detention and, in the absence of an available social worker (mental health officer), to give consent, there may be practical pressure on the relative to do so. This creates inevitable conflict of interest and conscience between carer and user (bearing in mind that suppressed perception of ill-health is a feature of some mental illness). The carer who is placed in the position of requesting care which the user actively resists has been party to the care which has failed. It is proposed to remove this conflict from new mental health legislation in Scotland since its undesirability for users, relatives and carers outweighs its convenience for statutory agencies (Millan 2001).

Personal property and personal care

The problems of managing the assets of persons requiring care has been an issue subsidiary to care for the many years in which mental health legislation has prevailed. It has become increasingly important in the context of means-tested benefits. However, the commercialisation of service delivery for those in need of care has brought the financial circumstances of the user into sharper focus. Direct charging for elements of care provision, direct payments to users or carers to secure care services, and charging for residential placements have been sources of great concern to individuals and to lobbying organisations. The Scottish Executive (1999) announced a commitment to funding personal care (a commitment not shared or adopted by the Westminster Government for users in England and Wales). The Executive, through its Central Research Unit, funded studies of opinion as to the need for and form of subsidy for personal care which have informed the Community Care and Health (Scotland) Bill now passed by the Scottish Parliament.

A clear area of conflict arises in relation to a family home or other asset that may have been perceived by carers as theirs of right in inheritance. Practices of transferring the property to the likely inheritors in advance of death are seen to have the effect of withdrawing the value of that property from consideration in means assessment for care cost liability. Sutherland (1999) neatly describes the potential legal difficulties in the context of paying for accommodation in Scotland, and Bransbury (1995) does so for England and Wales although both countries are subject to the same statutory rules concerning calculation of ability to pay. Alienation (giving ownership over to a third party) puts the user at risk of losing use of the property before alternative care is in place, since unless the user's continued occupation is secured, for example, by a lease from the new owner, the owner may simply dispose of it. There is also the possibility that those assessing liability for care costs deem the property to have been disposed of for the purposes of avoiding personal liability for costs (securing state funding in its place). While there are strict time limitations for striking down such transactions after they have occurred and recovering property from the recipient, there are no time limits on a decision to offer no aid, having deemed the property to be owned still by the user, who in turn is deemed to be able to recover it from those to whom it was conveyed with the alternative that they will act honourably to meet costs having succeeded to the asset. Such legal fictions may be justified in preventing alienation of assets to avoid liability for costs, but reliance upon the honour of recipients of the assets creates too great a risk for the actual care delivery to the user.

Anecdotal evidence and a flurry of cases of judicial review in which deemed ability to pay has been upheld suggest that the practice of dissipating assets to relatives and carers in order to avoid cost of residential care is quite prevalent. The introduction of funding for personal care in Scotland, while reducing the problem to some extent, will not eradicate it, nor will the simultaneous introduction of scope for deferral of payment until after death, since it is diminution of the potential estate that triggers alienation during life. The regulatory mechanisms for powers of attorney will only catch an alienation if it occurs after the power of attorney is activated in the event of incapacity. The protection of users is here in direct conflict with the interest of carers to protect a perceived right to inherit, but furthermore may be fuelled by an autonomous view of the user, that care is a matter for the state, funded by the tax and national insurance resource. This attitude is perhaps unsurprising given that the notion of private payment for publicly assessed care needs in old age or infirmity is scarcely a generation old. It would be extremely difficult to carry out qualitative research in this somewhat murky area, yet it is one in which the law develops without apparent regard to the fact that it is counter to values within personal caring, and research with a view to establishing a means of educating in this area should at least be attempted.

Duties of care and lack of care

Responsibilities in law towards those who are cared for is a matter of private and criminal law. The laws of tort in England and delict in Scotland impose a duty of care between carer and user and vice versa, breach of which (that is, failure in a duty of care) is actionable. Those who assume responsibilities as a carer, and in particular under a power of attorney, owe a fiduciary duty, that is a duty to perform the caring role in good faith for the benefit of the user, in a position of trust. This may be more exacting than service standards expected of a person giving care in the course of employment. Abuse may be picked up in the course of examination by a regulatory agency but even such an agency will rarely have the power to prohibit conduct (other than by a revised needs assessment removing the user from the adverse effect of the carer) nor to award compensation. While legal rights and duties in such situations are clear, and remedies exist in criminal law and in civil litigation, the accessibility of legal remedies may be poor. Difficulties in accessing legal advice, difficulties in communication that may hinder giving evidence, and the perception of the carer being more able to handle such processes than the user, make the reality much less clear than the legality. In the USA there is an ever-expanding research material and jurisprudence in the area of elder abuse which throws light upon an interesting and previously unspoken, area of law and practice. This area of commentary and jurisprudence is paradigmatic of the tensions that exist between carer and user. Laws exist in statute and at common law to deal with specific issues, but the underlying potential for conflict of interests and purposes between carer and user will not be prevented by the existence of laws. It is suggested that it will be dealt with only if faced and articulated in planning of care but in a manner which is non-judgemental and practical. If so faced it becomes part of a holistic and frank negotiation of a package of care.

Research studies have noted that needs assessment of user and carers call for a holistic approach (Murphy 1998), particularly where a child is involved. That is the ideal which can be sought in cases where the user can contribute to the care planning process. However in the substantial proportion of cases where the user is limited by memory loss, lack of power to communicate, or mental disorder, the all-inclusive process may not be achievable at a meaningful level. The issue of capacity for involvement by the user has been a major feature of the review of mental health legislation in England and Wales (Richardson 1999), raising more questions from the extensive body of research on capacity in consent and decision making than there can be answers (Dunn *et al.* 1998). In Scotland the issue is less acute in the mental health sphere, where it is proposed that tests based upon risk and assessment of illness are maintained. However the test of capacity or incapacity is still poorly understood among professionals (Atkinson and Patterson 2000; Gilmore *et al.* 1994).

Conclusions

The role of the carer, while increasingly recognised in law, is not well understood in the legal framework for the support and protection of users. Empirical evidence of carers' needs, assessed according to personal values and objective standards, should be compared and contrasted with the values, rights and wishes of users. A systematic and critical examination of legal and ethical risk in caring situations can be carried out only if there is better understanding of the complex and challenging frameworks within which users and carers are expected to function. The legal frameworks need to be juxtaposed with practical imperatives, and tensions identified and explored. We have care delivered privately in a private domain to presumptively autonomous adult by presumptively autonomous adult, but implemented in the name of the state and regulated according to public law descriptors. The depths of this challenging legal and ethical reality could be explored and mapped through empirical studies. Joint working in care delivery could become better informed. Users, and indeed carers, could be liberated by the knowledge that tensions thought to be personal to their caring situation are endorsed in many others. Principled decision making is only an advance if it can occur in a transparent, informed context. Until this complex interface of user and carer is described in an honest and critical manner, principles of law and ethics will be paper-thin protection for user or carer.

Notes

1. National Health Service and Community Care Act 1990 s55.

2. Mental Health Act 1983 s25B (2)(f), Mental Health (Scotland) Act 1984 s39B(2)(f) added by the Mental Health (Patients in the Community) Act 1995.

3. S1(1)b.

4. 1995 Act s1(3), 2000 Act s1(3),

5. The Employment Relations Act 1999 Part II which provides for the right to unpaid absence from work to deal with urgent or unexpected issues concerning dependents includes in addition to children, spouses and parents, a member of the same household (not residing there on a commercial arrangement), any person who reasonably relies on the employee for assistance if that person falls ill or is injured or assaulted, or to make arrangements for the provision of care in the event of illness or injury or for the provision of care that has been disrupted or terminated unexpectedly, Employment Relations Act 1996 as amended s57A(1), (3) & (4). The Inheritance (Provision of Family and Dependents) Act 1975 has allowed the court to look closely at the extent of financial dependence that a carer had upon a cared for person in *Hunt v Severs* 1994 2AC 350.

6. In the Adults with Incapacity (Scotland) Act 2000 there is reference to the 'primary carer', but this is defined merely to be the person or organisation primarily engaged in caring for the adult with incapacity, s87(1).

7. For example, a person caring for another for at least 35 hours per week is disregarded for the purpose of council tax for the house in which they live with the person being cared for.

8. Carers (Recognition and Services) Act 1995.

9. Human Rights Act 1998. An individual, or a commercial or voluntary organisation, may be acting as a public authority while contributing to delivery of a care package on behalf of a public authority.

References

Arber, S. and Evandrou, M. (1993) *Ageing, Independence and the Life Course.* London: Jessica Kingsley Publishers.

Atkinson, T. and Patterson, L. (2000) *Review of Literature relating to Mental Health Legislation.* Edinburgh: Scottish Executive Central Research Unit.

Bowes, A. and Dar, N. (2000) *Family Support and Community Care: A study of South Asian Older People.* (Social Work Research Findings No. 38). Edinburgh: Scottish Executive Central Research Unit.

Bransbury, L. (1995) 'Care in the Community.' In A. Griffiths and G. Roberts *The Law and Elderly People.* London: Routledge.

Churchill, R., Wall, S., Buchanan, A., Fahy, T., Hotopf, M. and Wessely, S. (1999) *A Systematic Review into the Use of the Mental Health Act, 1983.* London: Department of Health.

DoH (Department of Health) (1999) *Caring about Carers: A National Strategy for Carers.* London: Department of Health.

DoH (Department of Health) (2000) *Better Care, Higher Standards: A Charter for Long Term Care.* London: Deparment of Health.

Dunn, M., Wong, J., Clare, I. and Holland, I. (1998) Paper on Capacity for the Mental Health Act Review, Department of Health Mental Health Legislation Scoping Study, accessible at www.doh.gov.uk/mhar/mhascopstudy.htm

Eekelaar, J. and Pearl, D. (eds) (1989) *An Ageing World: Dilemmas and Challenges for Law and Social Policy.* Oxford: Clarendon Press.

Gilmore, C., Wood, G. and Rigby, J. (1994) 'Elderly patients and the Mental Health Act 1983.' *International Journal of Geriatric Psychiatry 9*, 10.

Griffiths, A. and Roberts, G. (1995) *The Law and Elderly People.* London: Routledge.

Kapp, M. (1991) 'Legal and ethical issues in family caregiving and the role of public policy.' *Home Health Care Services Quarterly 12*, 4, 5–28.

Law Commission for England and Wales (1995) *Mental Incapacity LC 231*. London: Law Commission.

Leontaridi, R. (2002) *Informal Care of the Elderly in Scotland and the UK (Health and Community Care Research Findings No. 8)*. Edinburgh: Scottish Executive Central Research Unit.

MacDonald, C. (1999) *Support at Home: Views of Older People about their Needs and Access to Services (Social Work Research Findings No. 35)*. Edinburgh: Scottish Executive Central Research Unit.

McHale, J. (1998) 'Confidentiality and Mental Health' for Review of Mental Health Act 1983, Department of Health available at www.doh.gov.uk/pub/docs/doh/mhapaper.pdf

McKay, C. and Patrick, H. (1995) *The Care Maze: The Law and Your Rights to Community Care in Scotland*. Edinburgh: Enable & SAMH.

Millan, B. (2001) *New Directions: Report on the Review of the Mental Health (Scotland) Act 1984*. Edinburgh: Scottish Executive.

Morris, J. (1993) *Independent Lives: Community Care and Disabled People*. London: Macmillan.

Murphy, T. (1998) 'Health Confidentiality in the Age of Talk.' In S. Sheddon and M. Thomson *Feminist Perspectives on Health Care Law.*

Petch, A., Cheetham, J., Fuller, R., MacDonald, C. and Myers, F. (1996) *Delivering Community Care: Initial Implementation of Care Management in Scotland (Social Work Research Findings No. 7)*. Edinburgh: Scottish Office, Central Research Unit.

Richardson, G. (1999) *Report, Review of the Mental Health Act 1983*, Report of the Expert Committee. London: Department of Health.

Scottish Executive (1999) *Strategy for Carers in Scotland*. Edinburgh: Scottish Executive.

Scottish Executive (2000) *The Same as You: A Review of Services for People with Learning Disabilities*. Edinburgh: Scottish Executive

Scottish Executive (2001) *Adults with Incapacity Act (Scotland) 2000 Code of Practice (x3)*. Edinburgh: Scottish Executive.

Scottish Law Commission (1995) *Incapable Adults (Scot Law Com No. 151)*. Edinburgh: Scottish Law Commission.

Stalker, K., Cadogan, L., Petric, M., Jones, C., and Murray, J. (1999) *'If you don't ask you don't get': Review of Services to People with Learning Disabilities: The Views of People who Use Services and their Carers*. Edinburgh: Scottish Executive Central Research Unit.

Stearns, S. and Butterworth, S. (2002) *Demand for, and Utilisation of, Personal-care Services for the Elderly (Health and Community Care Research Finding No. 7)*. Edinburgh: Scottish Executive Central Research Unit.

Sutherland, S. (1999) *With Respect to Old Age: Long term Care – Rights and Responsibilities*. Report of the Royal Commission on Long-Term Care, Cm 4192, London: HMSO.

Sutherland, E. (1999) *Child and Family Law.* Edinburgh: T&T Clark.

Wall, S., Hotopf, M., Wessely, S. and Churchill, R. (1999). 'Trends in the use of the Mental Health Act: England, 1984-96.' *British Medical Journal 318,* 1520–1521.

Wells, N. and Freer, C. (1988) *The Ageing Population: Burden or Challenge?* Basingstoke: Macmillan.

The Contributors

Hilary Arksey has worked as a research fellow in the Social Policy Research Unit at the University of York since 1995 when she was awarded a PhD in Independent Studies from Lancaster University. Her research projects include a study of carers and hospital discharge, a two-year study looking at the process and outcomes of assessment under the Carers (Recognition and Services) Act 1995 and an examination of employers' provisions for carers. Hilary's research interests are in the areas of informal care, employment and disability, and qualitative research methods.

Marian Barnes is Reader and Director of Social Research in the Department of Social Policy and Social Work at the University of Birmingham. She has previously worked at the Universities of Sheffield and Leeds and as a research officer in social services departments. Much of her work over the last 14 years has been on user involvement and user self-organisation in the context of health and social care. Her publications on this subject include *Care, Communities and Citizens* (Longman) and (with Ric Bowl) *Taking Over the Asylum: Empowerment and Mental Health* (Palgrave). She is currently researching community involvement and interagency partnerships in Health Action Zones, and is leading a project on public participation and social exclusion in the ESRC's Democracy and Participation research programme.

Rose Barton is the Professional Development, Education and Training Co-ordinator for Norfolk Mental Health Care NHS Trust where she works with service users, carers and practitioners to develop learning opportunities that support the modernisation of mental health services. Whilst employed as a lecturer at the University of East Anglia and the Open University her research and writing largely concerned carers' issues. This interest developed through her previous employment in residential childcare, police, probation, mental health and learning disability services and personal experience as an informal carer. She is assistant editor of the Blackwell Encyclopaedia of Social Work (2000) and contributed 'The carer's perspective' to Blackwell Companion to Social Work (2nd Edition, 2002).

Ann Brechin is a senior lecturer and sub-dean in the School of Health and Social Welfare at the Open University. Formerly a clinical psychologist, her teaching and research interests revolved around working with families with disabled children and adults with learning disabilities. A growing focus on relationships led to her subsequent research into difficulties in family care. This includes families with adult members with learning disability, older partners or parents with Alzheimers disease and children and young adults with M.E.

Susan Eley is a lecturer in the Department of Applied Social Science, University of Stirling, having worked previously as a research fellow at the University of Glasgow and at the MRC Medical Sociology Unit. She is a sociologist (BAEcon Manchester, MSc Stirling, PhD Glasgow) whose current research interests include young carers and service provision in health and social care. She has recently completed research with colleagues in the voluntary sector on children who care.

Gordon Grant is Professor of Cognitive Disabilities in the School of Nursing and Midwifery at the University of Sheffield, and Doncaster and South Humber Healthcare NHS Trust. Gordon was previously Co-Director of the Centre for Social Policy Research and Development at the University of Wales, Bangor. His research interests include family care giving across the lifespan, resilience and coping in families, violent suicide, the social inclusion of disadvantaged groups, and the scope of participatory action research. In his present role he is working towards developing research capacity within nursing and professions allied to medicine, and the fostering of research commissioning systems that include people with learning disabilities.

Liz Lloyd is a lecturer at the School for Policy Studies, University of Bristol. Her research experience is in community care and health. Her research and publications have been focused primarily on the experiences of older people and carers. An ongoing interest is the health and well-being of older people at the end of life and the significance of this for understanding the nature of dependency. Liz heads an interdisciplinary team researching Significant Life Events in people aged 80 plus. She is also part of a team that is developing a model of ageing for application in the sphere of social housing.

Elinor Nicholas is a research fellow at the Social Policy Research Unit, University of York. She is a qualified social worker (CQSW) and has an MA in Social Services Planning. Previous posts in social services include Project Development Manager and Training Officer, Community Care. Her research interests include outcomes in social care, with a particular focus on carers of adults, and care management. She has led development work on outcomes-focused assessment and review for carers, in partnership with services, and is currently co-ordinating a research-practice network aiming to support implementation of outcomes approaches.

Hazel Qureshi is Professor of Social Care and Assistant Director of the Social Policy Research Unit, University of York. After an initial period in social care practice in the statutory and voluntary sectors, she has pursued a full-time career in research. She was awarded her PhD for a study of parents caring for adult children with severe learning difficulties and challenging behaviour. Her research interests are in the perspectives of service users and their families, service evaluation, and achieving an outcome focus in social care practice. She has published widely on social care, including *The Caring Relationship* (with Alan Walker) and *Outcomes of Community Care for Service Users and Carers* (with Andrew Nocon).

Paul Ramcharan is a senior lecturer in the Department of Mental Health and Learning Disability Nursing in the School of Nursing and Midwifery at the University of Sheffield. He was previously involved in research relating to family care giving and people with learning disabilities in Wales under the All Wales Strategy. More recently he has been involved in the Community Fund supported Advocating for Work and Care project in collaboration with Wigan and Leigh Crossroads Care Scheme and Add-a-Voice. This work examines how carers seek to enter employment and, in doing this, the effect on their families and on those for whom they care.

Helen Rogers is currently a research fellow in the Department of Social Policy and Social Work and an Associate Director of the Inter-disciplinary Centre for Mental Health at the University of Birmingham. She has substantial experience as a practitioner, middle and senior manager in the field of mental health and substance misuse. Her research and writing interests centre on partnership working, not only between organisations but also between organisations and service users and carers.

Margaret L. Ross is a senior lecturer in Law and Deputy Head of the Law School, University of Aberdeen. She is Vice-Chair of the Mental Welfare Commission for Scotland and is also Curator *ad litem*, reporting officer and a safeguarder in sheriff courts. She was previously a partner in a private legal practice, part-time chair of child support appeal tribunals and lay member, then chair of Grampian Research Ethics Committee. Her research interests include evidence, procedures, mental health, ethics and complaints, and alternative dispute resolution.

Kirsten Stalker is a senior research fellow at the Social Work Research Centre, University of Stirling. She previously worked at the Norah Fry Research Centre, University of Bristol. Her main research interests relate to social models of disability, and user choice and participation, and she has published widely in that area. Kirsten has been awarded research grants from various bodies including the Economic and Social Research Council, the Department of Health, the Scottish Executive, the Joseph Rowntree Foundation and the Nuffield Foundation.

June Stein has worked as a research fellow at the School of Health and Social Welfare at the Open University where her main field of research was adult protection following on her earlier research in the area of adults with learning disability and sexual abuse. Her work with carers led to Nuffield Foundation funding for research into the problems of nursing students with sole child care responsibilities. Her current interests are in patterns of offending of people with mental health problems. She now works as a freelance researcher as well as undertaking teaching and training.

Bridget Whittell was, at the time of writing this chapter, a research officer in the Department of Mental Health and Learning Disability Nursing in the School of Nursing and Midwifery at the University of Sheffield. Bridget has a PhD in social policy and her research work and interests cover family care giving, learning disability issues, advocacy and empowerment. Bridget has just completed a project in Wigan called Advocating for Work and Care that is about examining the issues involved for carers who want to find employment.

Subject Index

Author Index